Shild and T

Story & Art by Alexis E. Fajardo

Cover colors by Brian Kolm
Interior colors by Alexis E. Fajardo and Jose Flores

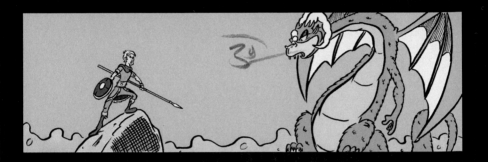

Before Beowulf and Grendel there was Shild and the Dragon!

Find out what happens when Beowulf's great-grandfather Shild encounters the Dragon in the wilds of Daneland and learns about a world filled with monsters, slayers, and his special place in it!

"Shild and the Dragon" is the first story in a new series of stand-alone, *Kid Beowulf Eddas* – stories exploring the rich world of characters from the Kid Beowulf universe.

The Kid Beowulf Eddas

Print ISBN 978-0-9909505-0-9

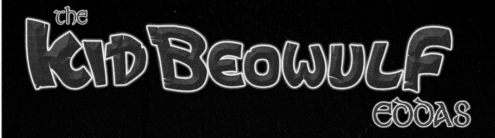

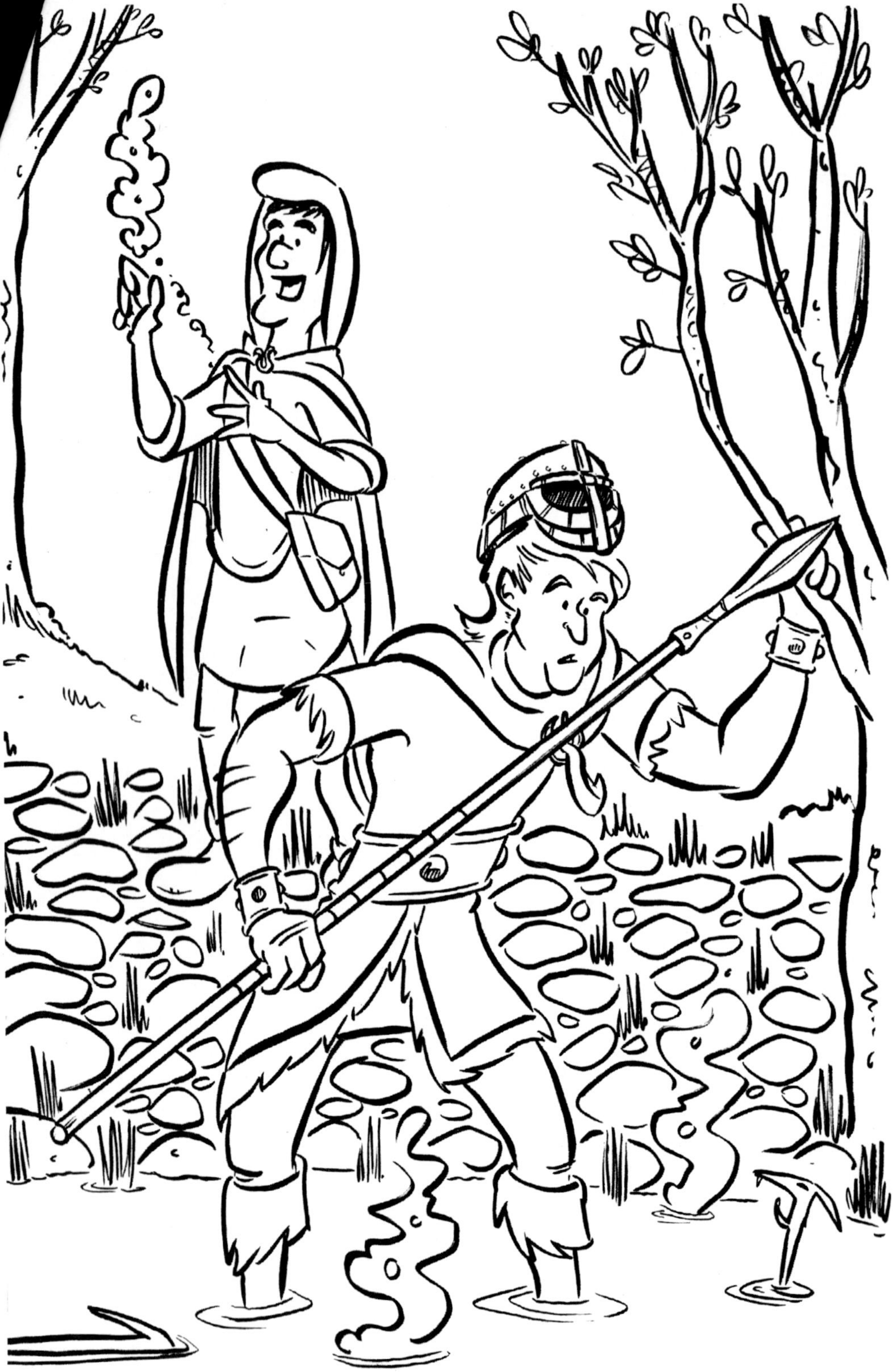

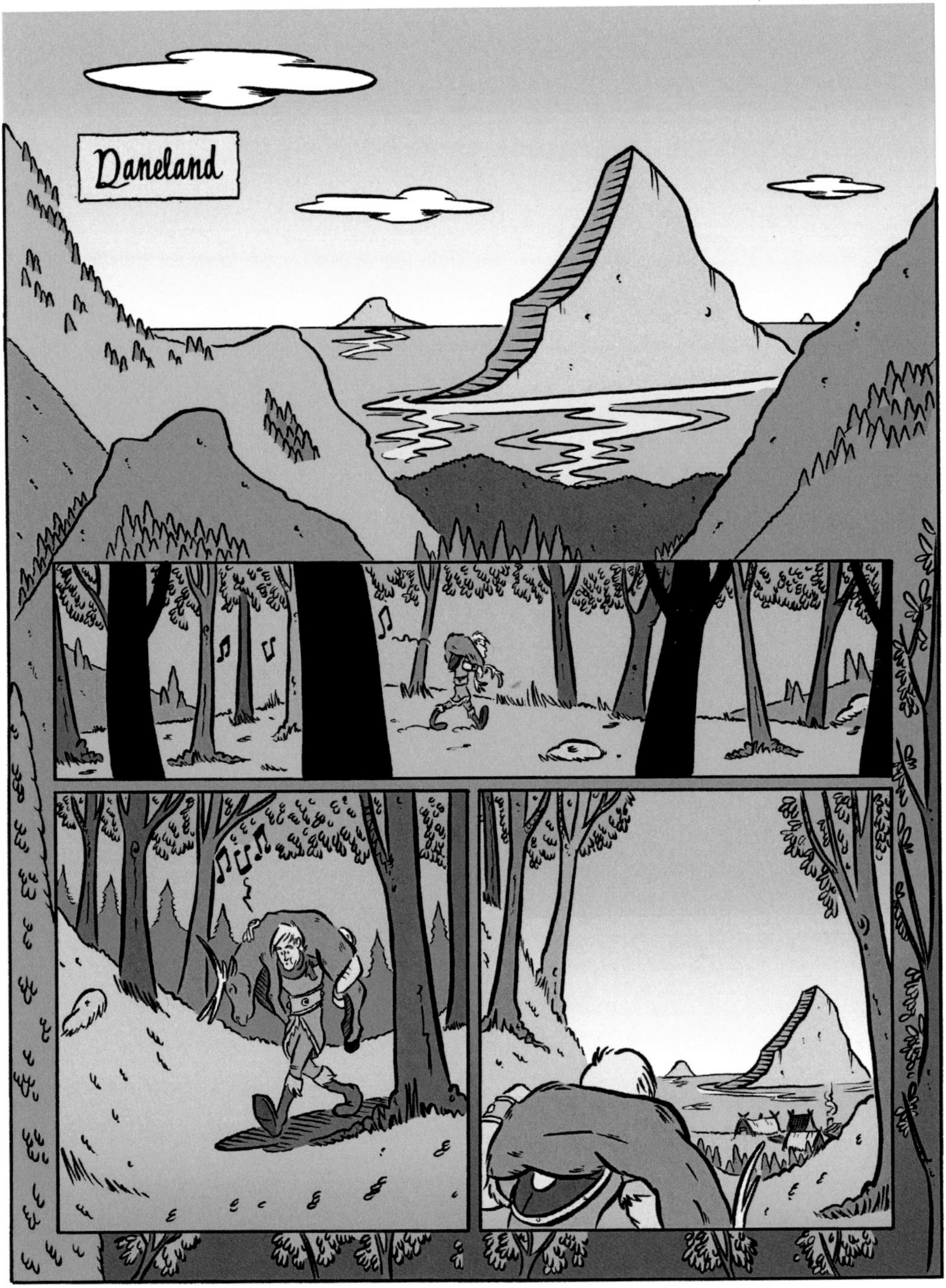
Daneland

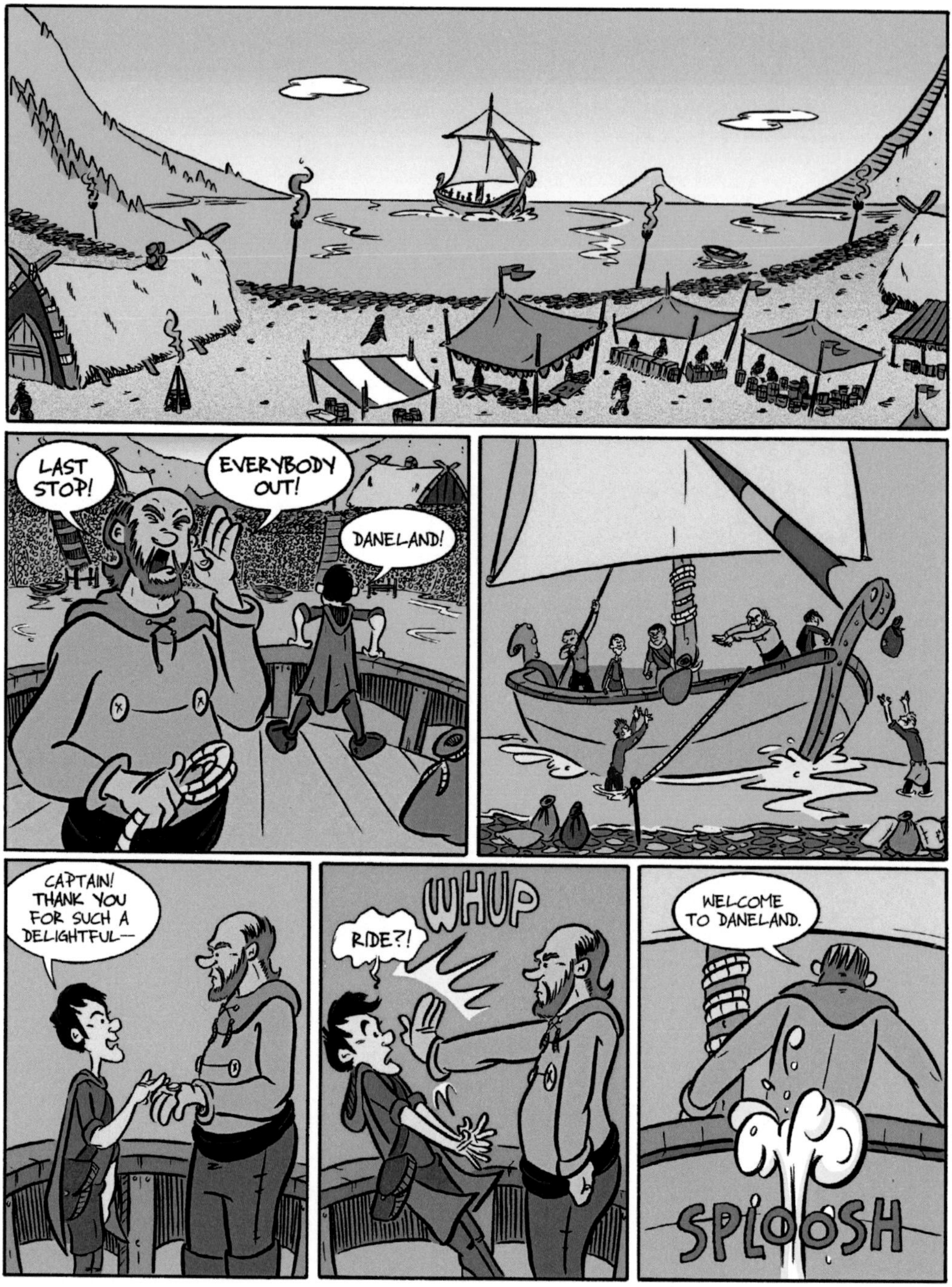
LAST STOP!
EVERYBODY OUT!
DANELAND!
CAPTAIN! THANK YOU FOR SUCH A DELIGHTFUL—
RIDE?!
WHUP
WELCOME TO DANELAND.
SPLOOSH

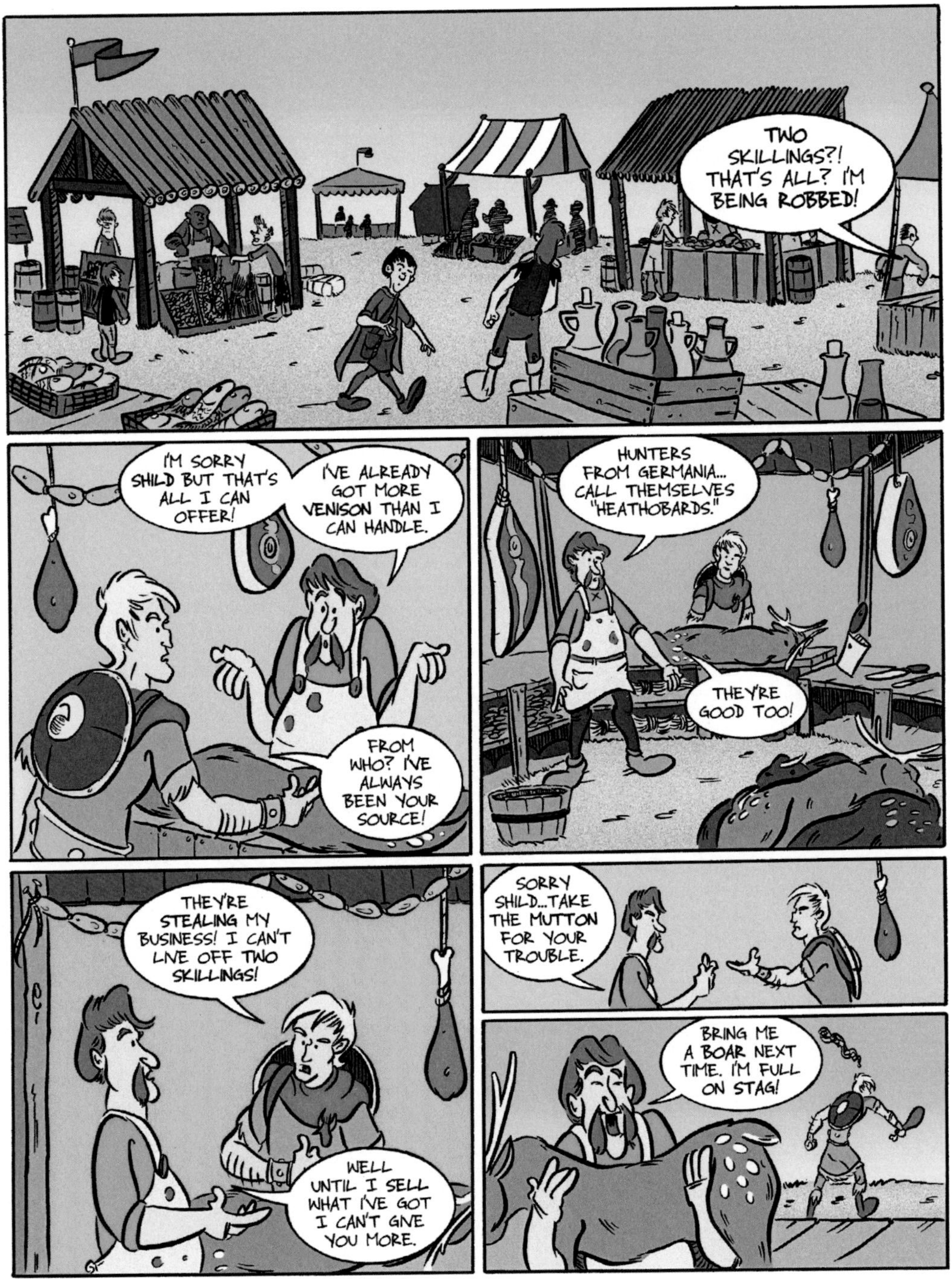
TWO SKILLINGS?! THAT'S ALL? I'M BEING ROBBED!
I'M SORRY SHILD BUT THAT'S ALL I CAN OFFER!
I'VE ALREADY GOT MORE VENISON THAN I CAN HANDLE.
FROM WHO? I'VE ALWAYS BEEN YOUR SOURCE!
HUNTERS FROM GERMANIA... CALL THEMSELVES "HEATHOBARDS."
THEY'RE GOOD TOO!
THEY'RE STEALING MY BUSINESS! I CAN'T LIVE OFF TWO SKILLINGS!
WELL UNTIL I SELL WHAT I'VE GOT I CAN'T GIVE YOU MORE.
SORRY SHILD...TAKE THE MUTTON FOR YOUR TROUBLE.
BRING ME A BOAR NEXT TIME. I'M FULL ON STAG!

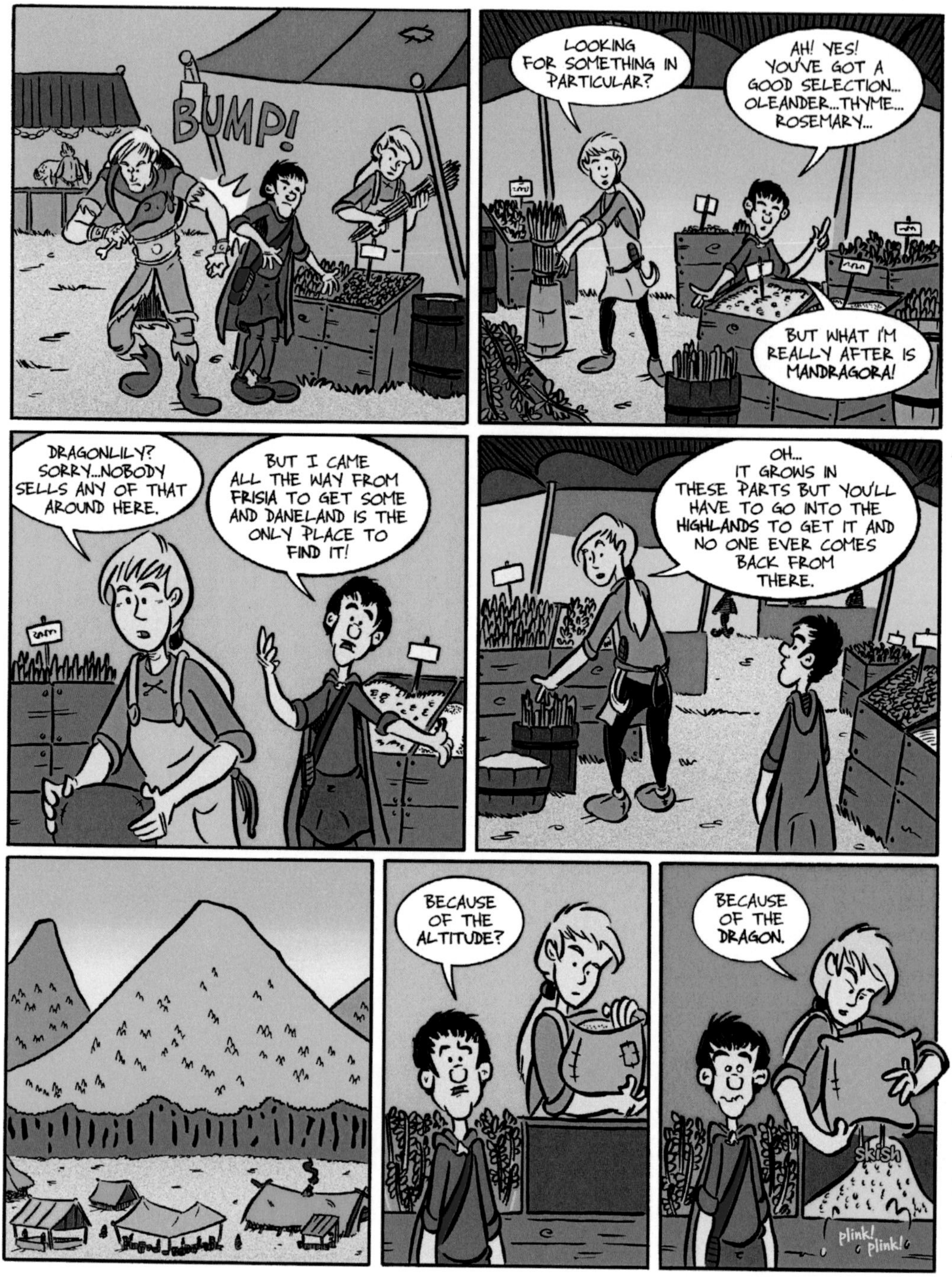
BUMP!
LOOKING FOR SOMETHING IN PARTICULAR?
AH! YES! YOU'VE GOT A GOOD SELECTION... OLEANDER...THYME... ROSEMARY...
BUT WHAT I'M REALLY AFTER IS MANDRAGORA!
DRAGONLILY? SORRY...NOBODY SELLS ANY OF THAT AROUND HERE.
BUT I CAME ALL THE WAY FROM FRISIA TO GET SOME AND DANELAND IS THE ONLY PLACE TO FIND IT!
OH... IT GROWS IN THESE PARTS BUT YOU'LL HAVE TO GO INTO THE HIGHLANDS TO GET IT AND NO ONE EVER COMES BACK FROM THERE.
BECAUSE OF THE ALTITUDE?
BECAUSE OF THE DRAGON.
SKISH
plink! plink!

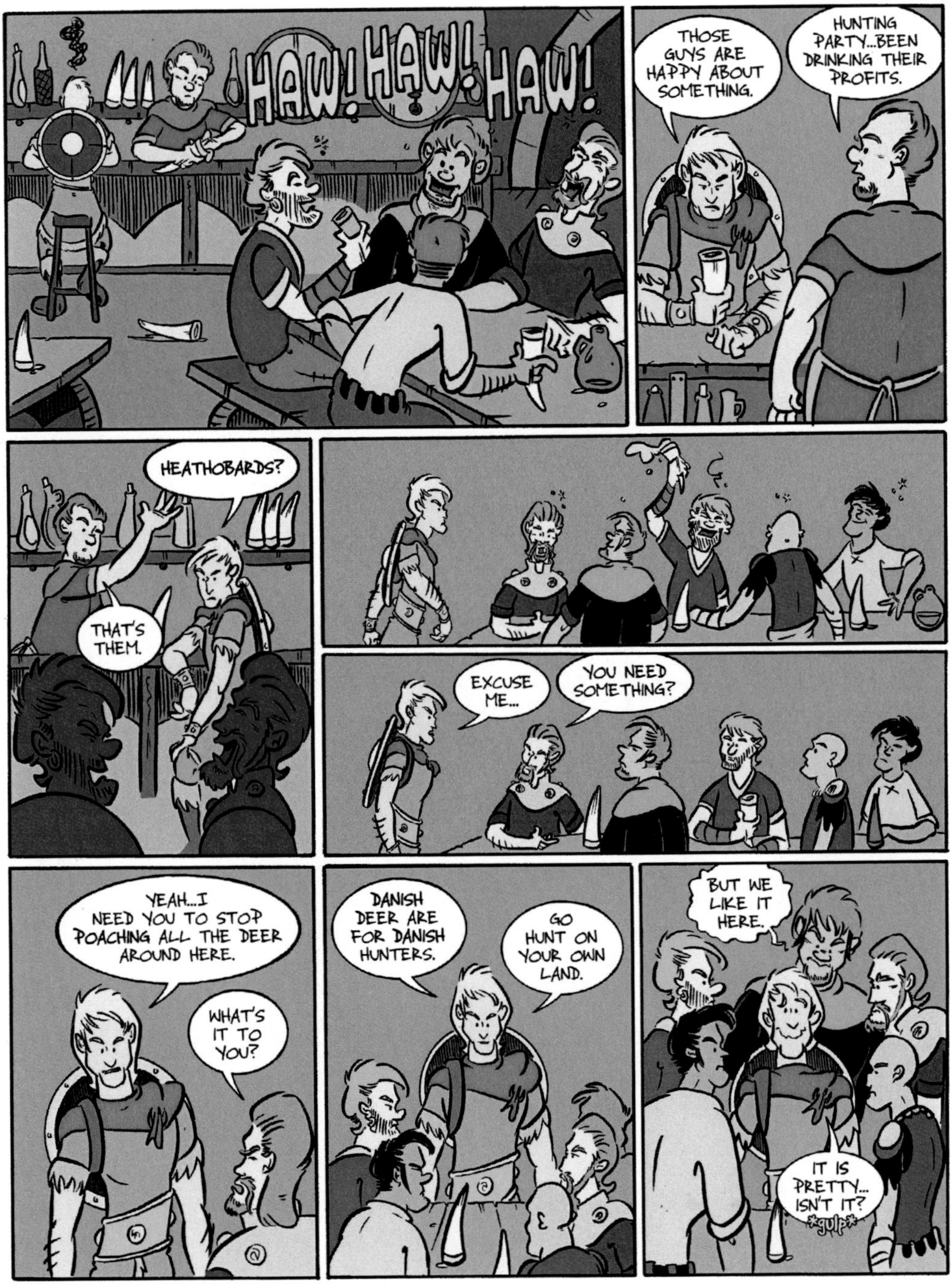
HAW! HAW! HAW!
THOSE GUYS ARE HAPPY ABOUT SOMETHING.
HUNTING PARTY...BEEN DRINKING THEIR PROFITS.
HEATHOBARDS?
THAT'S THEM.
EXCUSE ME...
YOU NEED SOMETHING?
YEAH...I NEED YOU TO STOP POACHING ALL THE DEER AROUND HERE.
WHAT'S IT TO YOU?
DANISH DEER ARE FOR DANISH HUNTERS.
GO HUNT ON YOUR OWN LAND.
BUT WE LIKE IT HERE.
IT IS PRETTY... ISN'T IT?
gulp

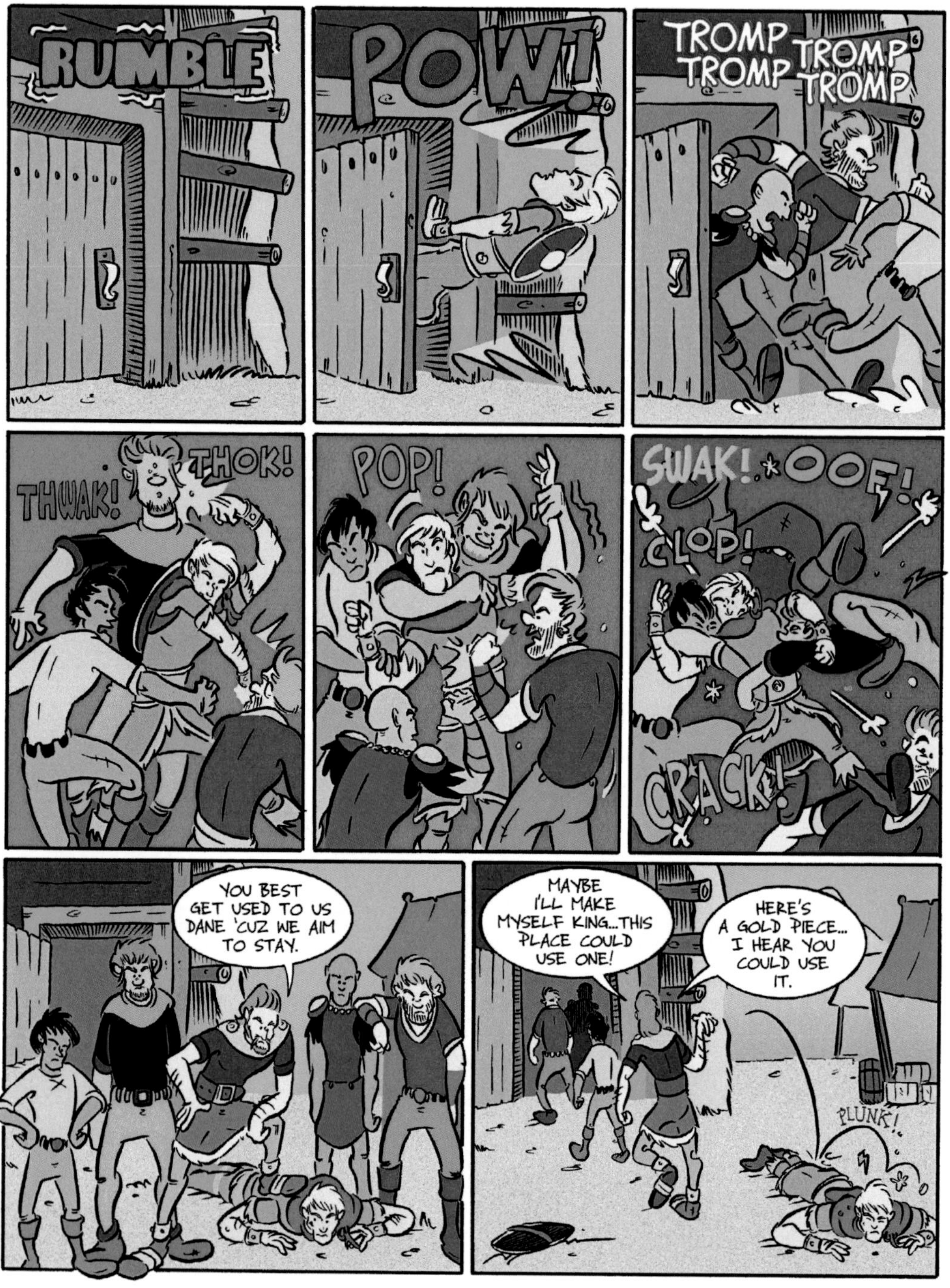
RUMBLE
POW!
TROMP TROMP TROMP TROMP
THWAK!
THOK!
POP!
SWAK!
OOF!
CLOP!
CRACK!
YOU BEST GET USED TO US DANE 'CUZ WE AIM TO STAY.
MAYBE I'LL MAKE MYSELF KING...THIS PLACE COULD USE ONE!
HERE'S A GOLD PIECE... I HEAR YOU COULD USE IT.
PLUNK!

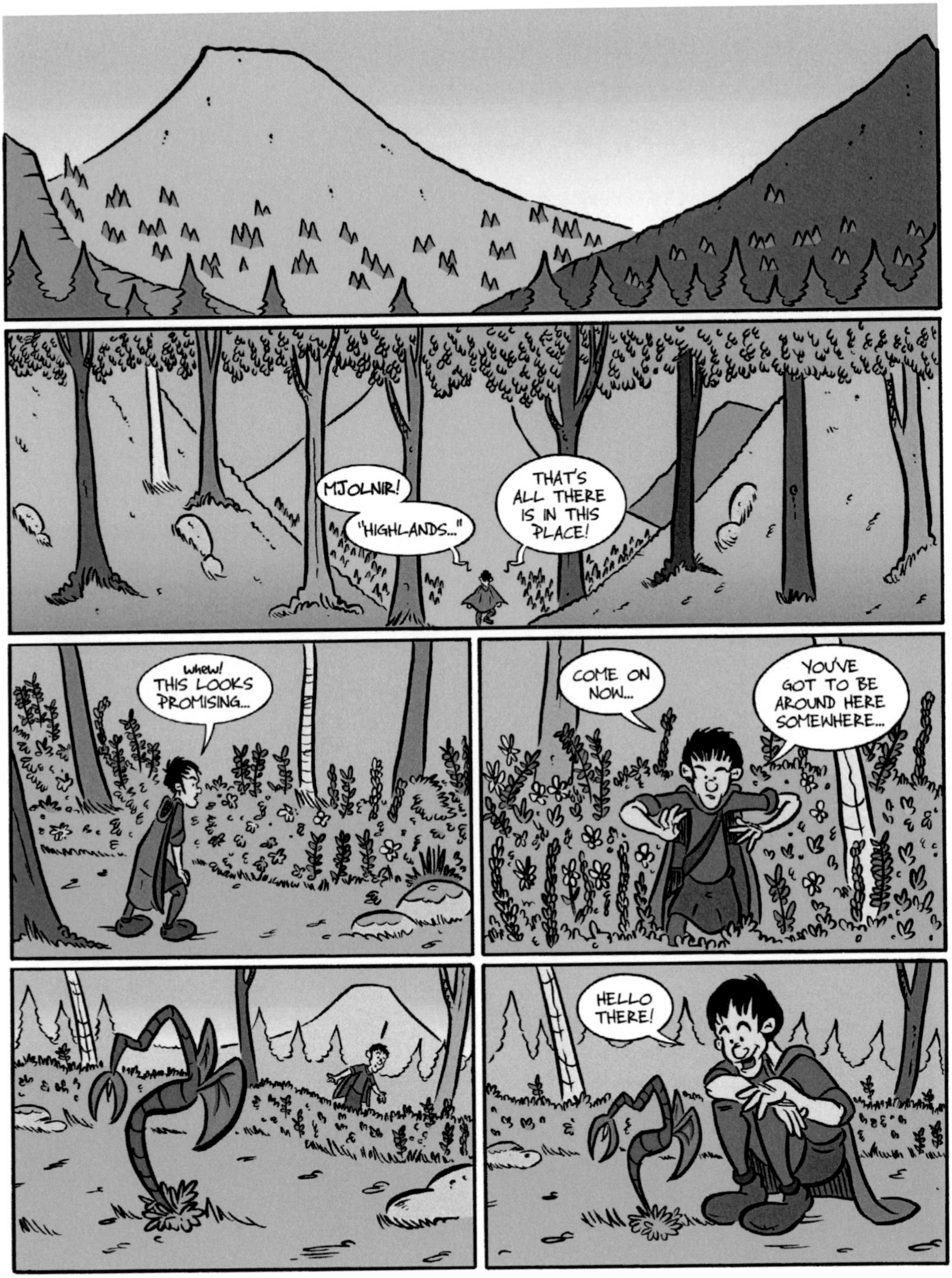
MJOLNIR!
"HIGHLANDS..."
THAT'S ALL THERE IS IN THIS PLACE!
whew! THIS LOOKS PROMISING...
COME ON NOW...
YOU'VE GOT TO BE AROUND HERE SOMEWHERE...
HELLO THERE!

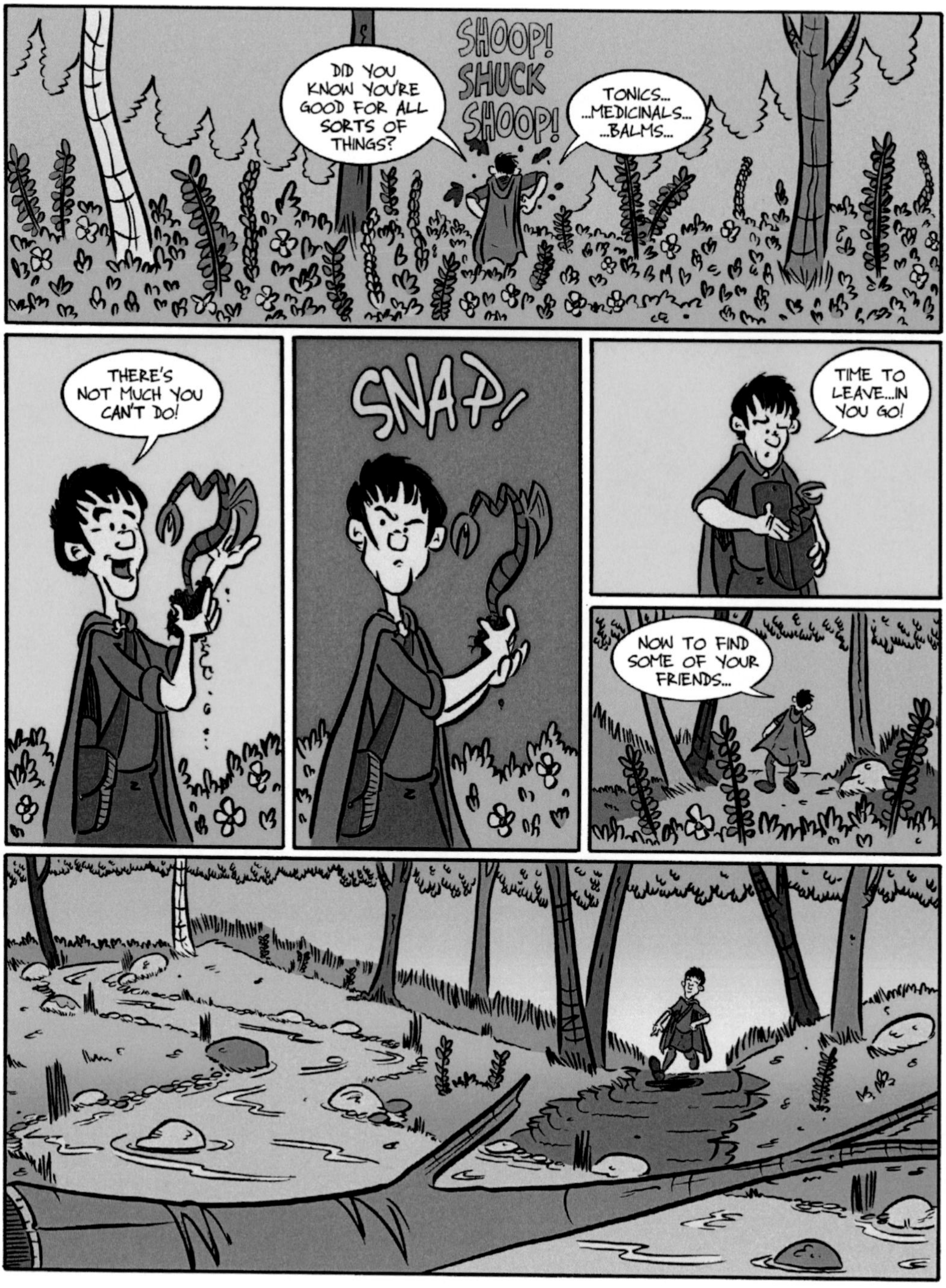
DID YOU KNOW YOU'RE GOOD FOR ALL SORTS OF THINGS?
SHOOP! SHUCK SHOOP!
TONICS... ...MEDICINALS... ...BALMS...
THERE'S NOT MUCH YOU CAN'T DO!
SNAP!
TIME TO LEAVE...IN YOU GO!
NOW TO FIND SOME OF YOUR FRIENDS...

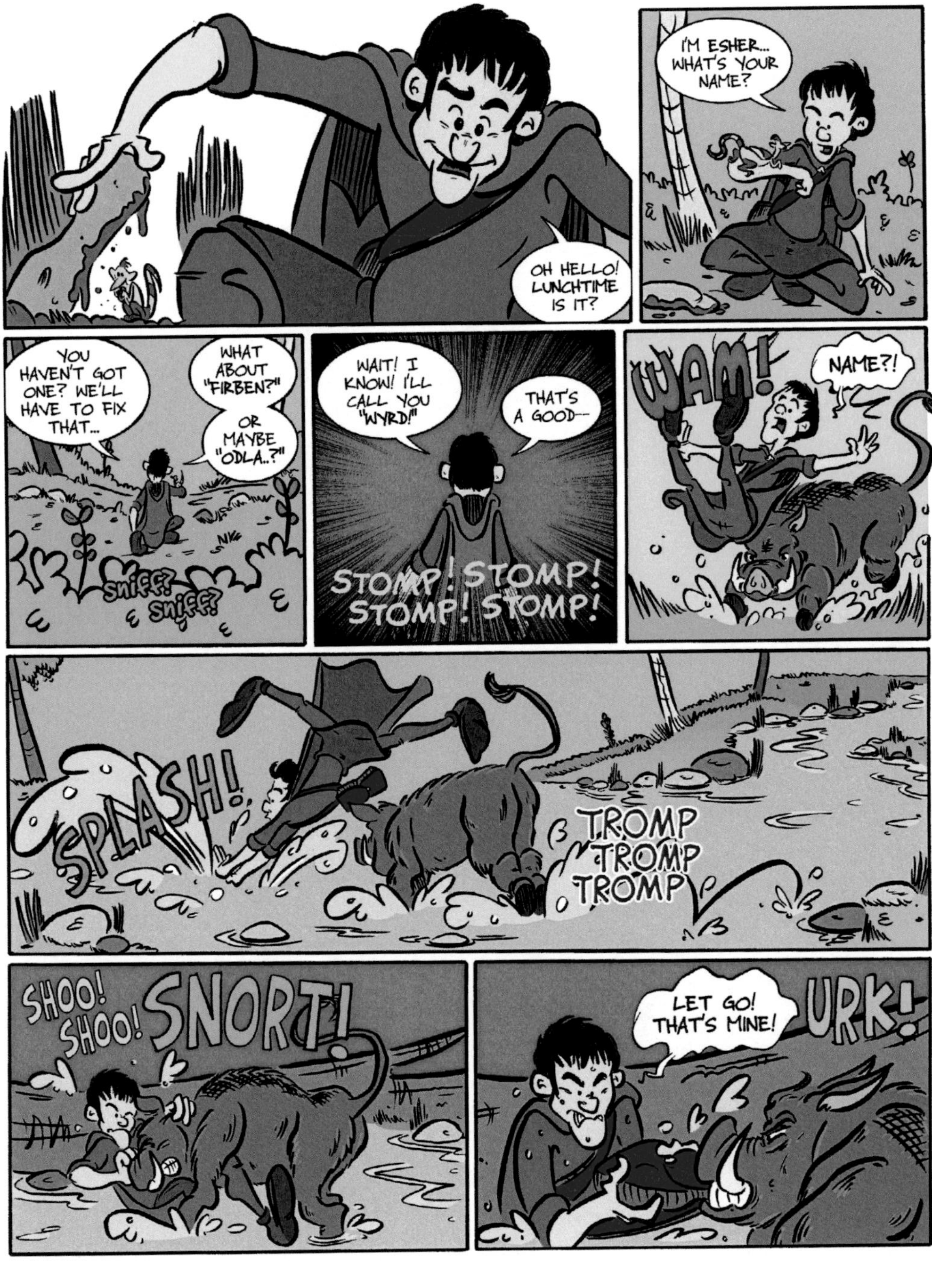
OH HELLO! LUNCHTIME IS IT?
I'M ESHER... WHAT'S YOUR NAME?
YOU HAVEN'T GOT ONE? WE'LL HAVE TO FIX THAT...
WHAT ABOUT "FIRBEN?"
OR MAYBE "ODLA..?"
sniff? sniff?
WAIT! I KNOW! I'LL CALL YOU "WYRD!"
THAT'S A GOOD---
STOMP! STOMP! STOMP! STOMP!
WAM!
NAME?!
SPLASH!
TROMP TROMP TROMP
SHOO! SHOO!
SNORT!
LET GO! THAT'S MINE!
URK!

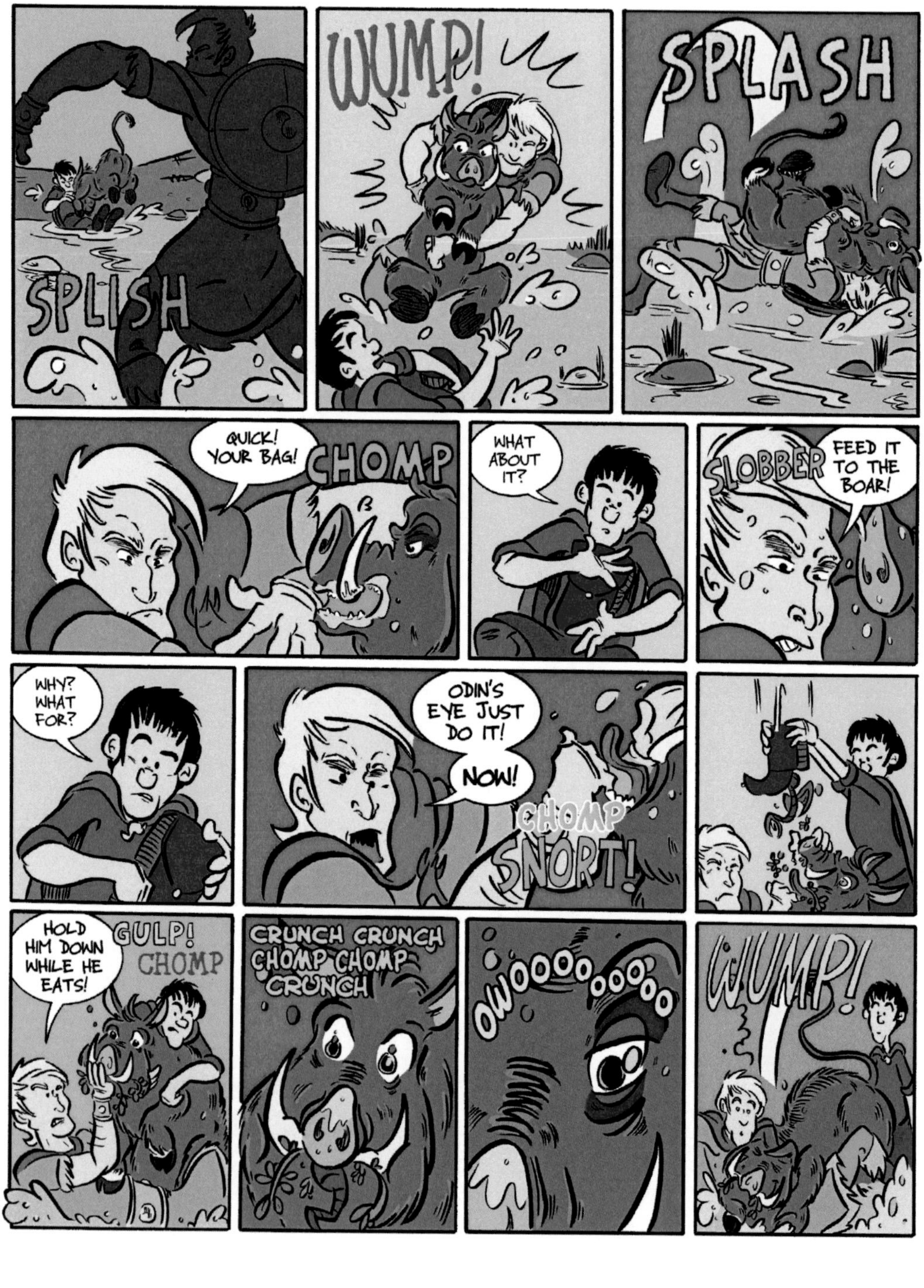
SPLISH
WUMP!
SPLASH
QUICK! YOUR BAG!
CHOMP
WHAT ABOUT IT?
SLOBBER
FEED IT TO THE BOAR!
WHY? WHAT FOR?
ODIN'S EYE JUST DO IT!
NOW!
CHOMP
SNORT!
HOLD HIM DOWN WHILE HE EATS!
GULP!
CHOMP
CRUNCH CRUNCH
CHOMP CHOMP
CRUNCH
OWOOOOOOOOO
WUMP!

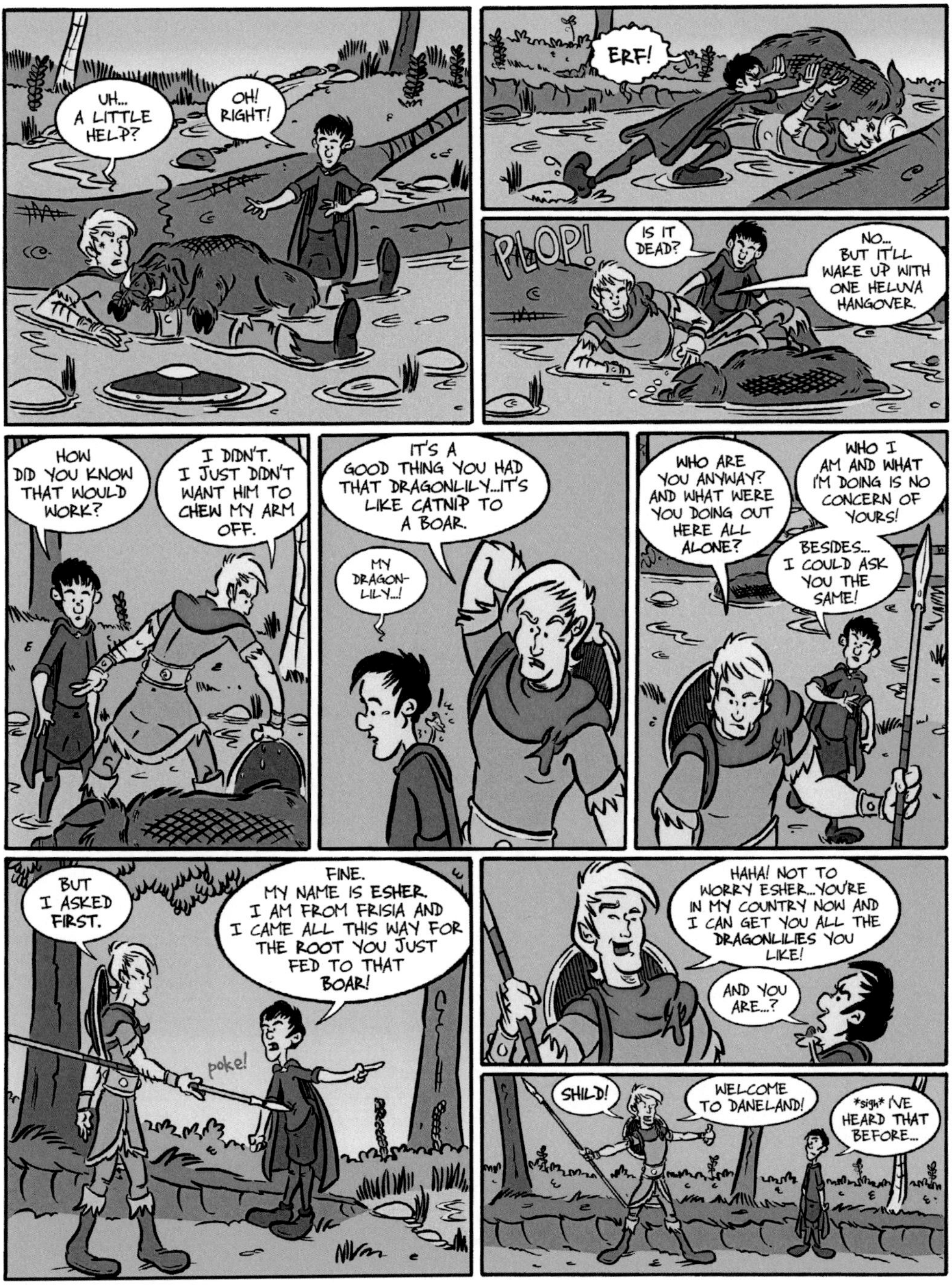
UH... A LITTLE HELP?
OH! RIGHT!
ERF!
PLOP!
IS IT DEAD?
NO... BUT IT'LL WAKE UP WITH ONE HELUVA HANGOVER.
HOW DID YOU KNOW THAT WOULD WORK?
I DIDN'T. I JUST DIDN'T WANT HIM TO CHEW MY ARM OFF.
IT'S A GOOD THING YOU HAD THAT DRAGONLILY...IT'S LIKE CATNIP TO A BOAR.
MY DRAGON-LILY...!
WHO ARE YOU ANYWAY? AND WHAT WERE YOU DOING OUT HERE ALL ALONE?
WHO I AM AND WHAT I'M DOING IS NO CONCERN OF YOURS!
BESIDES... I COULD ASK YOU THE SAME!
BUT I ASKED FIRST.
FINE. MY NAME IS ESHER. I AM FROM FRISIA AND I CAME ALL THIS WAY FOR THE ROOT YOU JUST FED TO THAT BOAR!
poke!
HAHA! NOT TO WORRY ESHER...YOU'RE IN MY COUNTRY NOW AND I CAN GET YOU ALL THE DRAGONLILIES YOU LIKE!
AND YOU ARE...?
SHILD!
WELCOME TO DANELAND!
sigh I'VE HEARD THAT BEFORE...

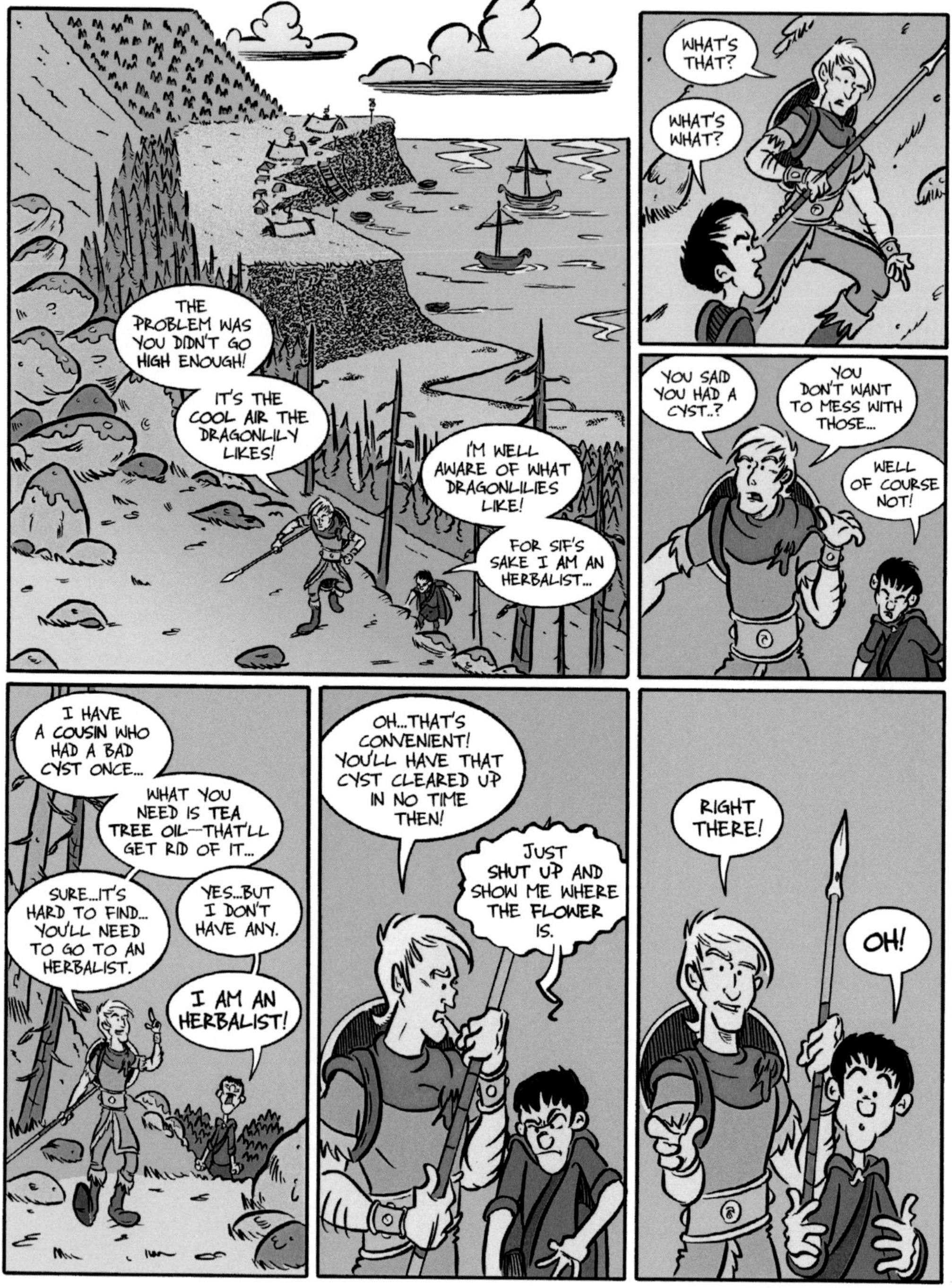
THE PROBLEM WAS YOU DIDN'T GO HIGH ENOUGH!
IT'S THE COOL AIR THE DRAGONLILY LIKES!
I'M WELL AWARE OF WHAT DRAGONLILIES LIKE!
FOR SIF'S SAKE I AM AN HERBALIST...
WHAT'S THAT?
WHAT'S WHAT?
YOU SAID YOU HAD A CYST..?
YOU DON'T WANT TO MESS WITH THOSE...
WELL OF COURSE NOT!
I HAVE A COUSIN WHO HAD A BAD CYST ONCE...
WHAT YOU NEED IS TEA TREE OIL—THAT'LL GET RID OF IT...
SURE...IT'S HARD TO FIND... YOU'LL NEED TO GO TO AN HERBALIST.
YES...BUT I DON'T HAVE ANY.
I AM AN HERBALIST!
OH...THAT'S CONVENIENT! YOU'LL HAVE THAT CYST CLEARED UP IN NO TIME THEN!
JUST SHUT UP AND SHOW ME WHERE THE FLOWER IS.
RIGHT THERE!
OH!

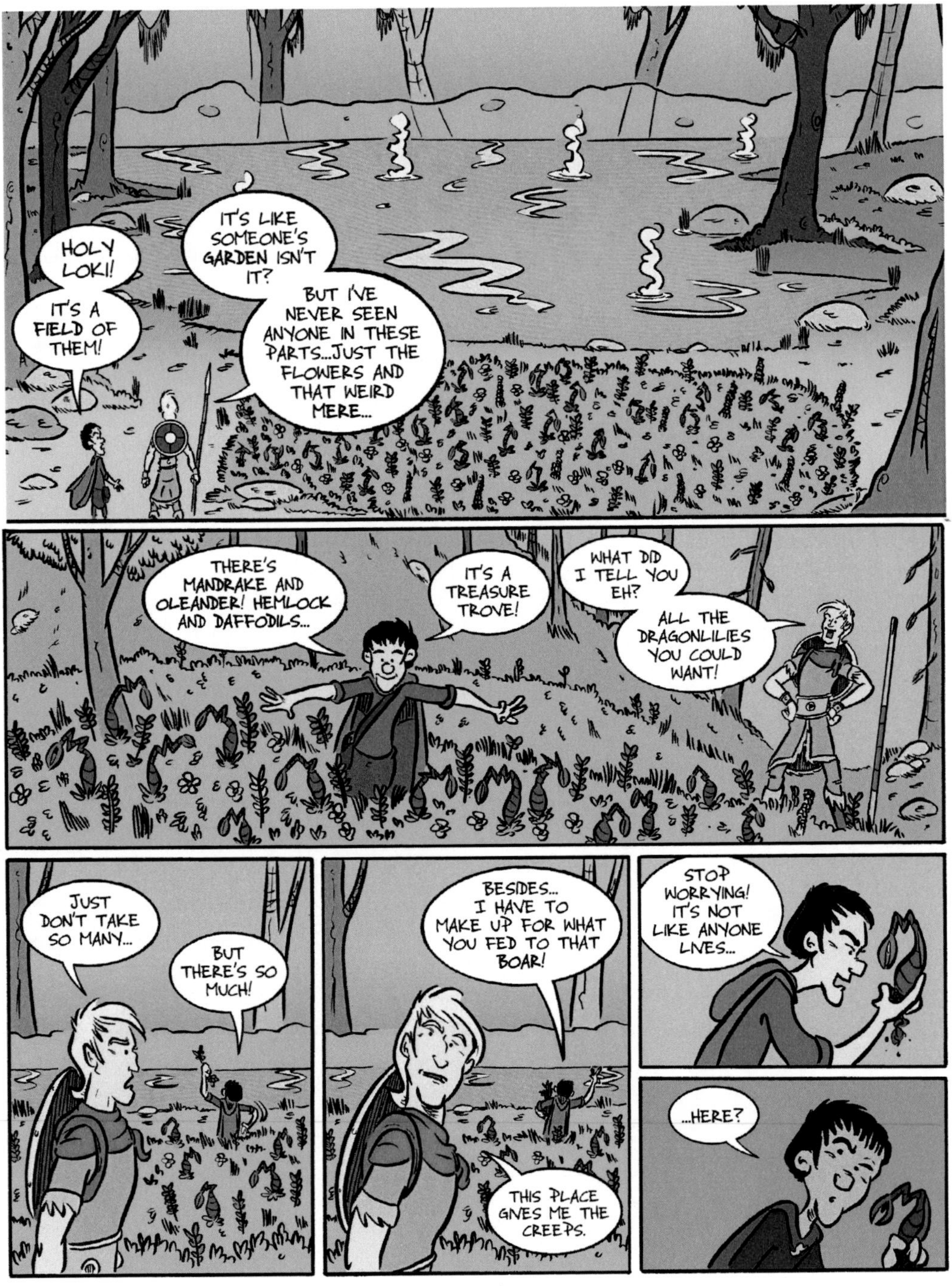
HOLY LOKI!
IT'S A FIELD OF THEM!
IT'S LIKE SOMEONE'S GARDEN ISN'T IT?
BUT I'VE NEVER SEEN ANYONE IN THESE PARTS...JUST THE FLOWERS AND THAT WEIRD MERE...
THERE'S MANDRAKE AND OLEANDER! HEMLOCK AND DAFFODILS...
IT'S A TREASURE TROVE!
WHAT DID I TELL YOU EH?
ALL THE DRAGONLILIES YOU COULD WANT!
JUST DON'T TAKE SO MANY...
BUT THERE'S SO MUCH!
BESIDES... I HAVE TO MAKE UP FOR WHAT YOU FED TO THAT BOAR!
THIS PLACE GIVES ME THE CREEPS.
STOP WORRYING! IT'S NOT LIKE ANYONE LIVES...
...HERE?

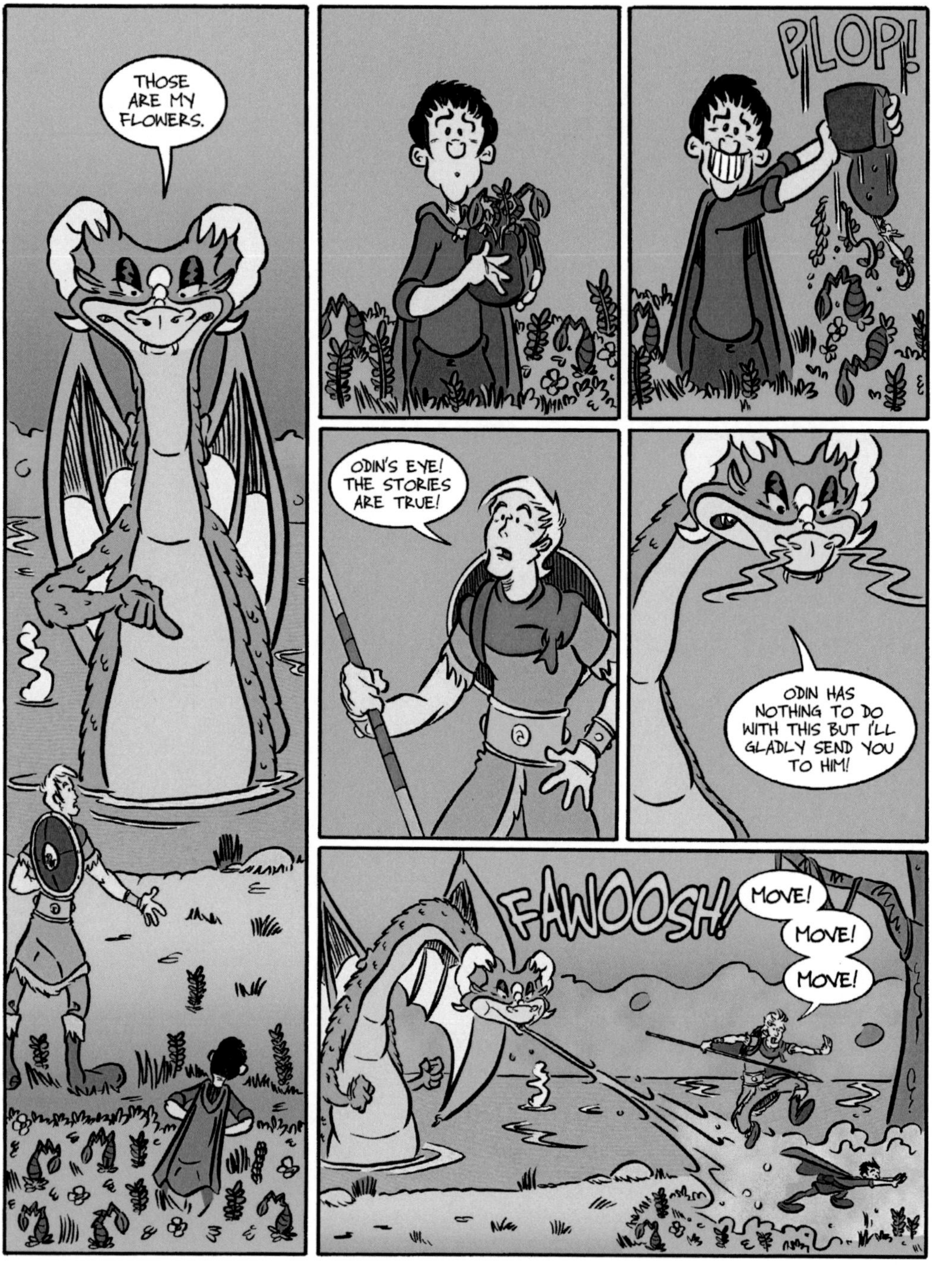
THOSE ARE MY FLOWERS.
PLOP!
ODIN'S EYE! THE STORIES ARE TRUE!
ODIN HAS NOTHING TO DO WITH THIS BUT I'LL GLADLY SEND YOU TO HIM!
FAWOOSH!
MOVE!
MOVE!
MOVE!

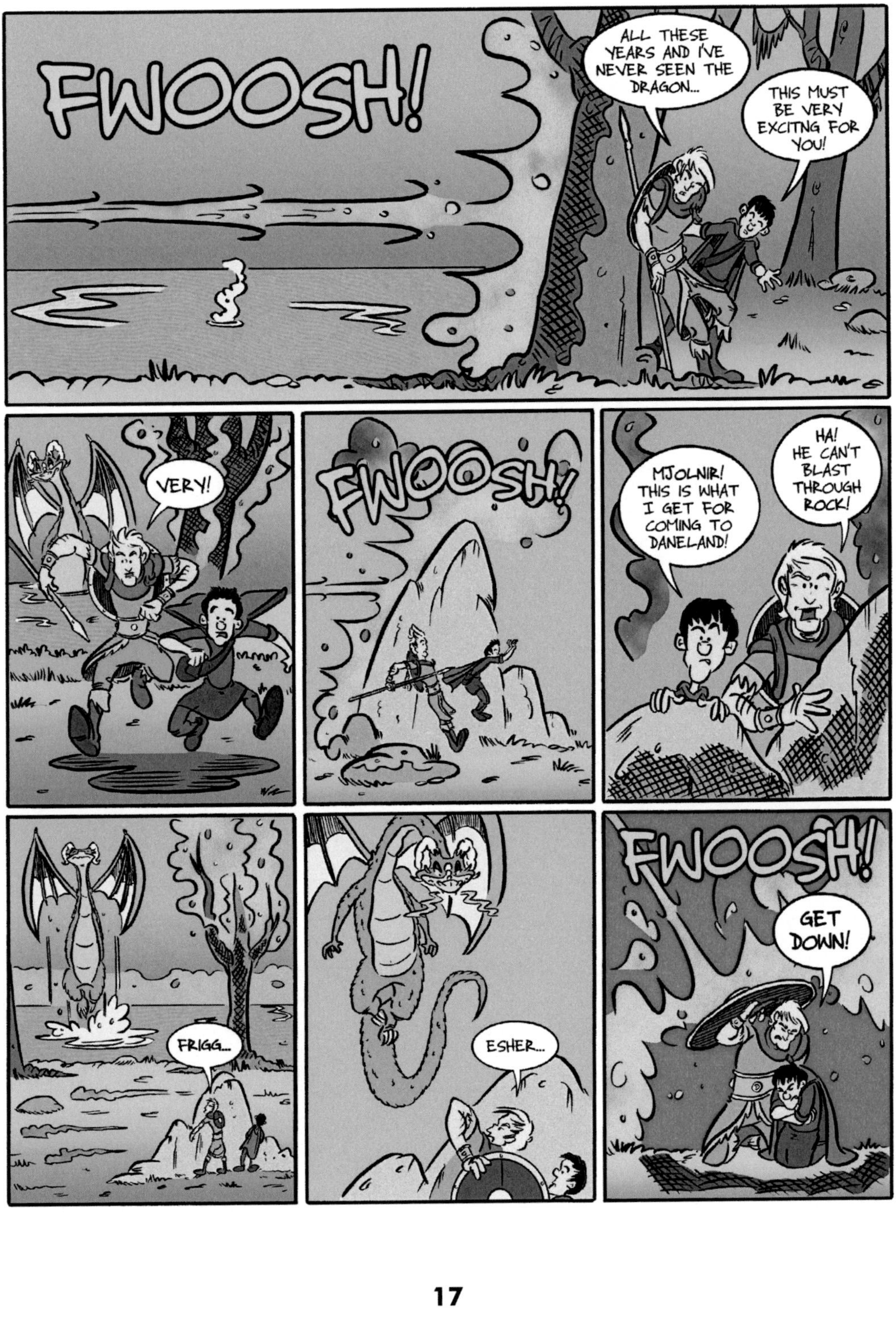
FWOOSH!
ALL THESE YEARS AND I'VE NEVER SEEN THE DRAGON...
THIS MUST BE VERY EXCITNG FOR YOU!
VERY!
FWOOSH!
MJOLNIR! THIS IS WHAT I GET FOR COMING TO DANELAND!
HA! HE CAN'T BLAST THROUGH ROCK!
FRIGG...
ESHER...
FWOOSH!
GET DOWN!

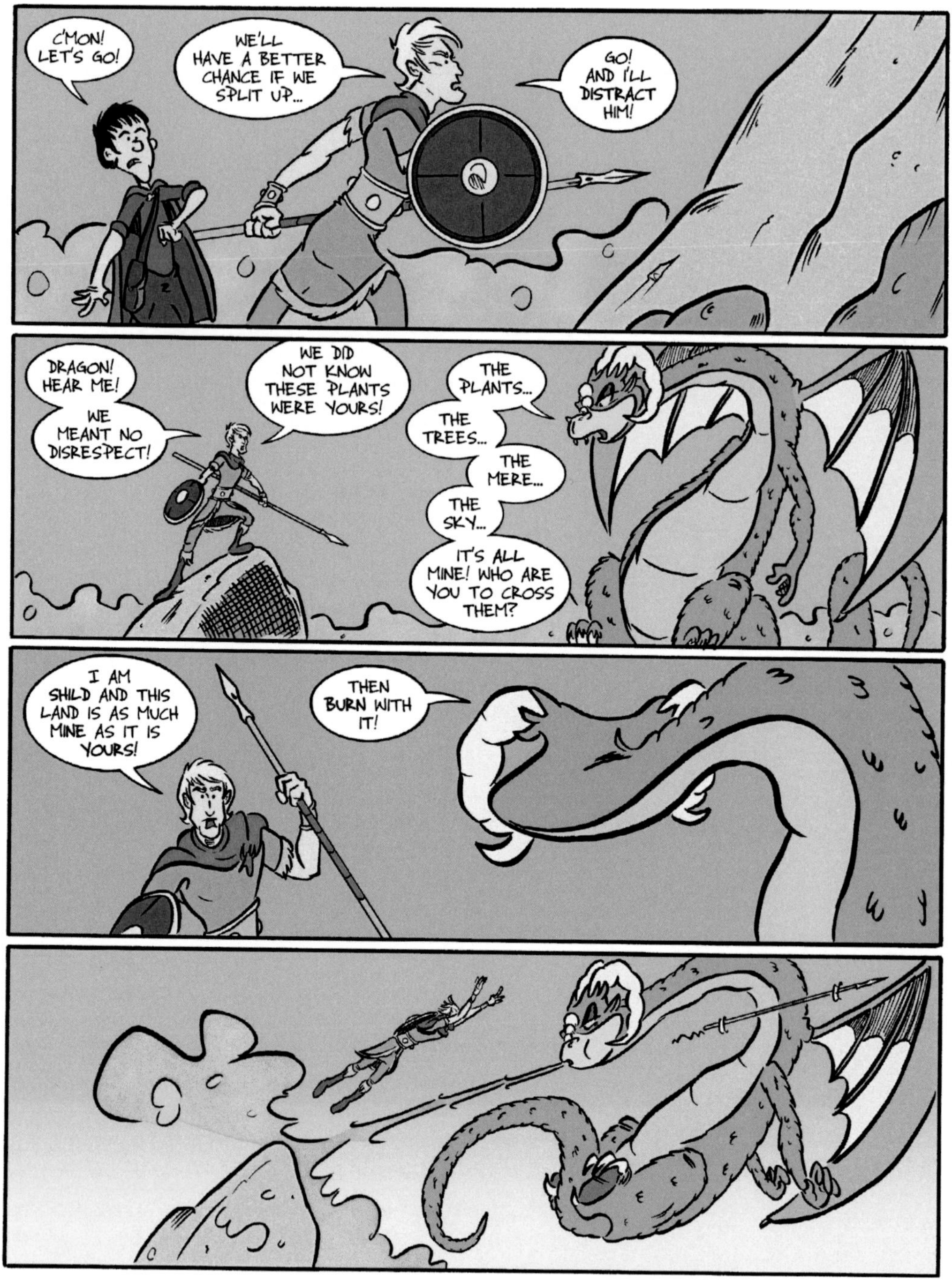
C'MON! LET'S GO!
WE'LL HAVE A BETTER CHANCE IF WE SPLIT UP...
GO! AND I'LL DISTRACT HIM!
DRAGON! HEAR ME!
WE MEANT NO DISRESPECT!
WE DID NOT KNOW THESE PLANTS WERE YOURS!
THE PLANTS...
THE TREES...
THE MERE...
THE SKY...
IT'S ALL MINE! WHO ARE YOU TO CROSS THEM?
I AM SHILD AND THIS LAND IS AS MUCH MINE AS IT IS YOURS!
THEN BURN WITH IT!

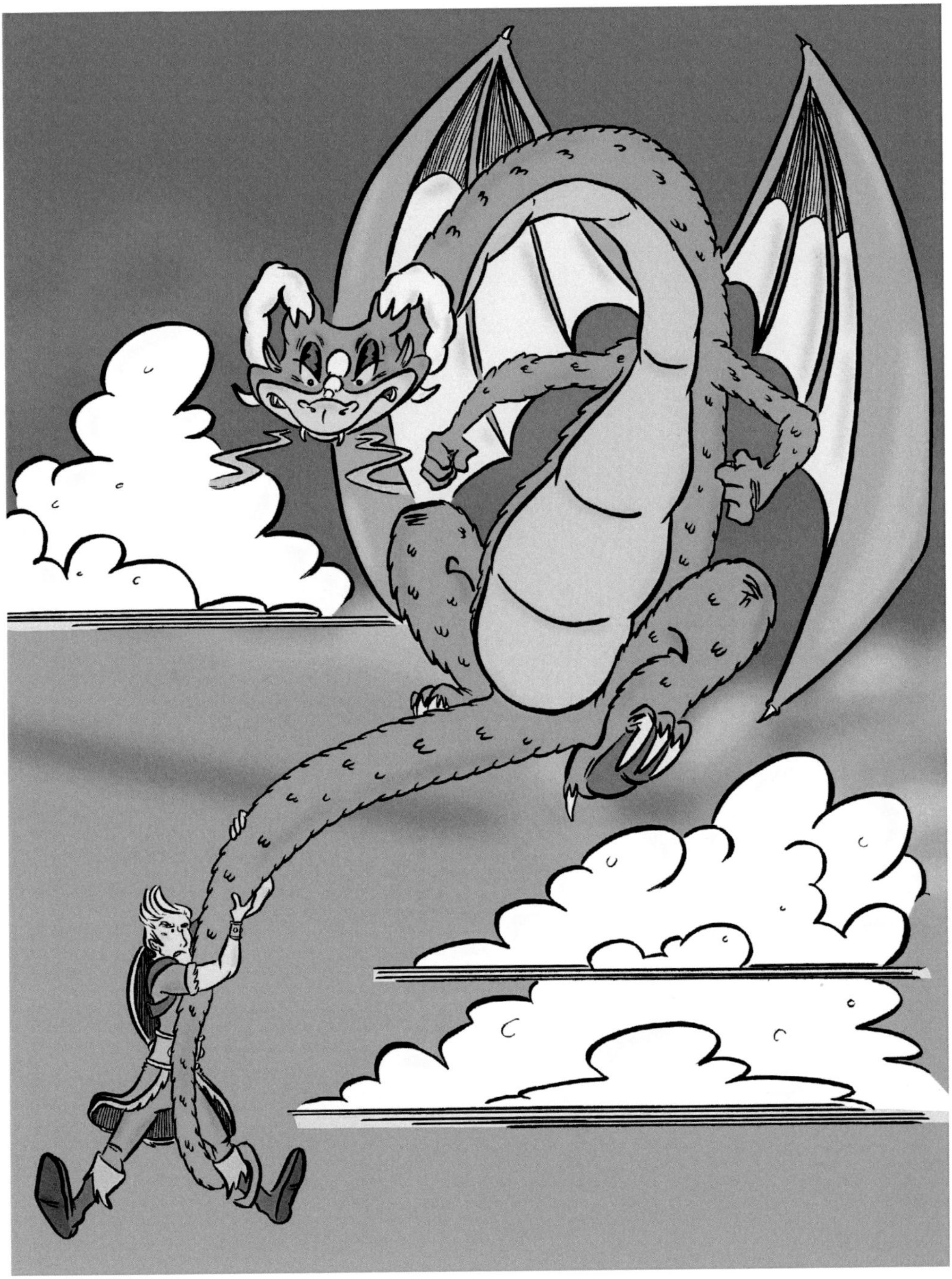

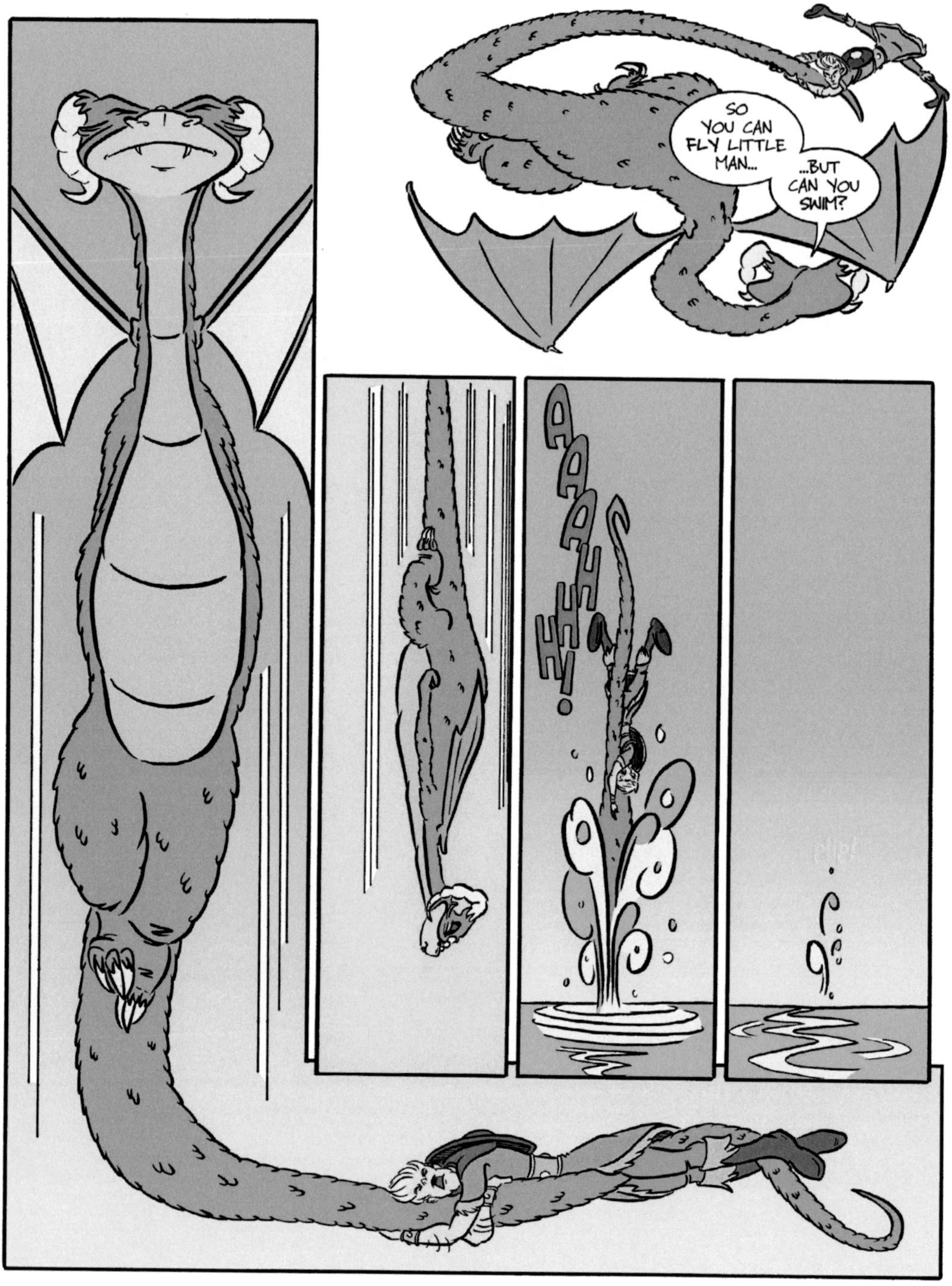
SO YOU CAN FLY LITTLE MAN...
...BUT CAN YOU SWIM?
AAAHHH!

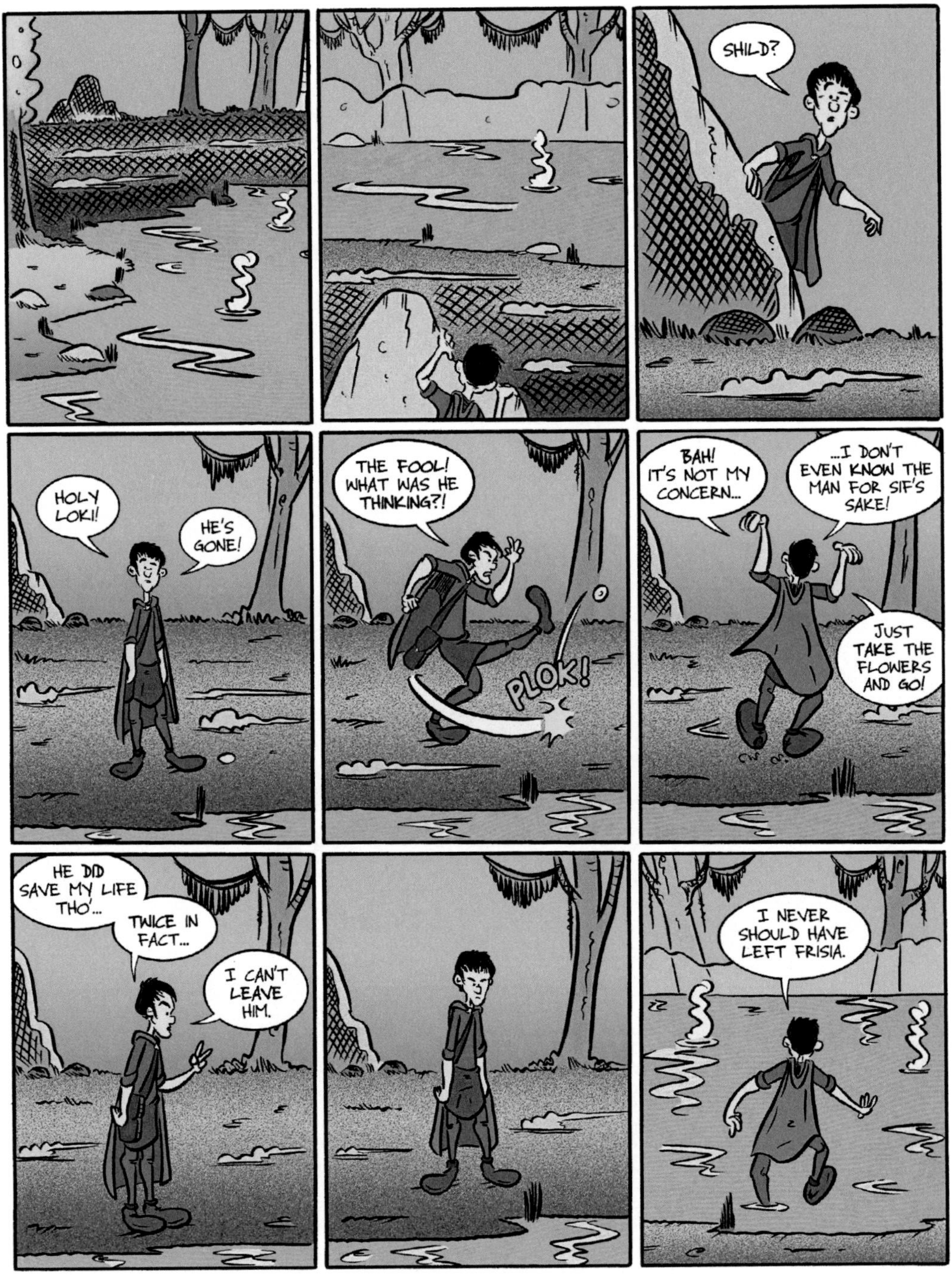
SHILD?
HOLY LOKI!
HE'S GONE!
THE FOOL! WHAT WAS HE THINKING?!
PLOK!
BAH! IT'S NOT MY CONCERN...
...I DON'T EVEN KNOW THE MAN FOR SIF'S SAKE!
JUST TAKE THE FLOWERS AND GO!
HE DID SAVE MY LIFE THO'...
TWICE IN FACT...
I CAN'T LEAVE HIM.
I NEVER SHOULD HAVE LEFT FRISIA.

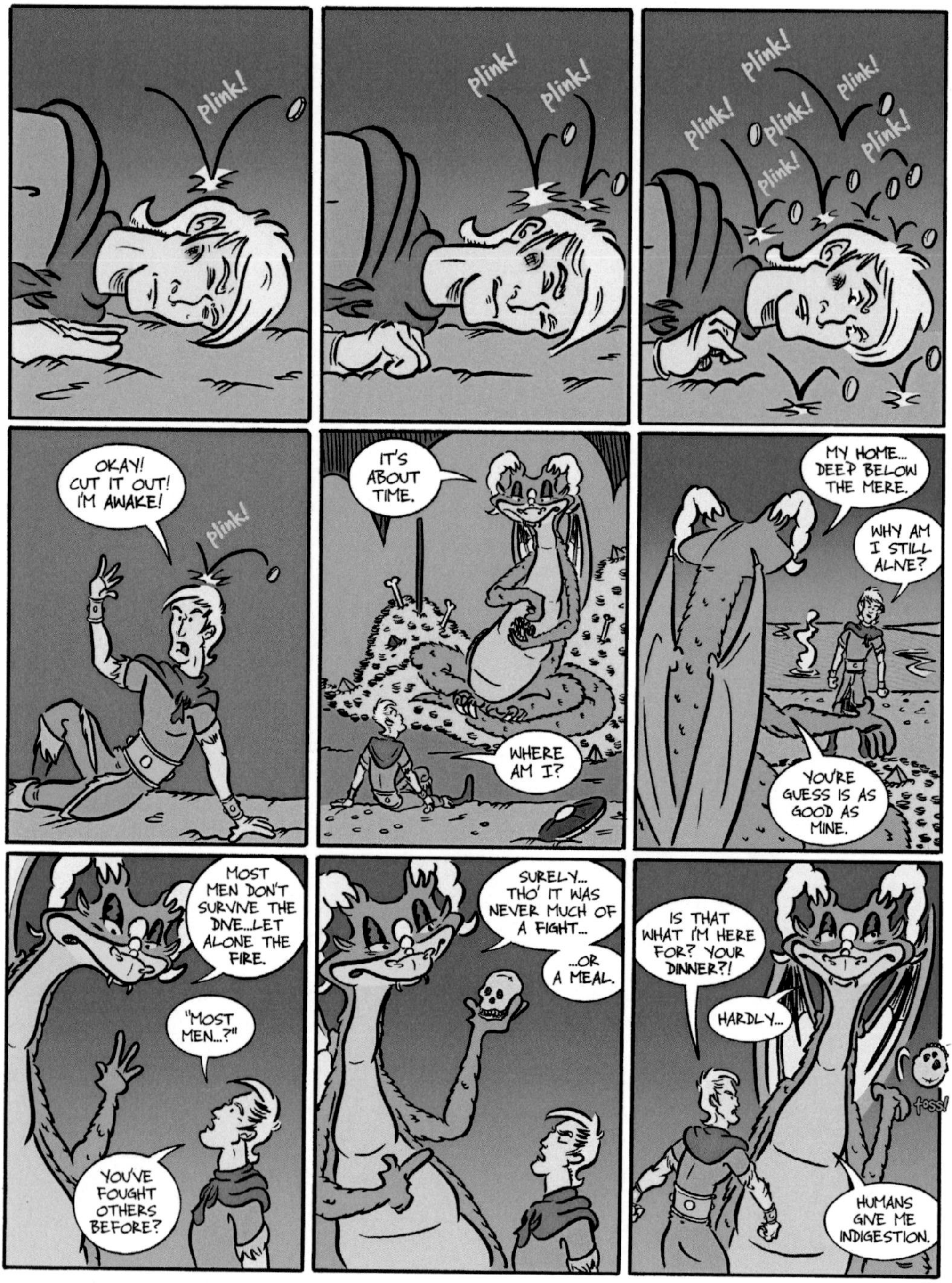
plink!
plink!
plink!
plink!
plink!
plink!
plink!
plink!
plink!
OKAY! CUT IT OUT! I'M AWAKE!
plink!
IT'S ABOUT TIME.
WHERE AM I?
MY HOME... DEEP BELOW THE MERE.
WHY AM I STILL ALIVE?
YOU'RE GUESS IS AS GOOD AS MINE.
MOST MEN DON'T SURVIVE THE DIVE...LET ALONE THE FIRE.
"MOST MEN...?"
YOU'VE FOUGHT OTHERS BEFORE?
SURELY... THO' IT WAS NEVER MUCH OF A FIGHT...
...OR A MEAL.
IS THAT WHAT I'M HERE FOR? YOUR DINNER?!
HARDLY...
toss!
HUMANS GIVE ME INDIGESTION.

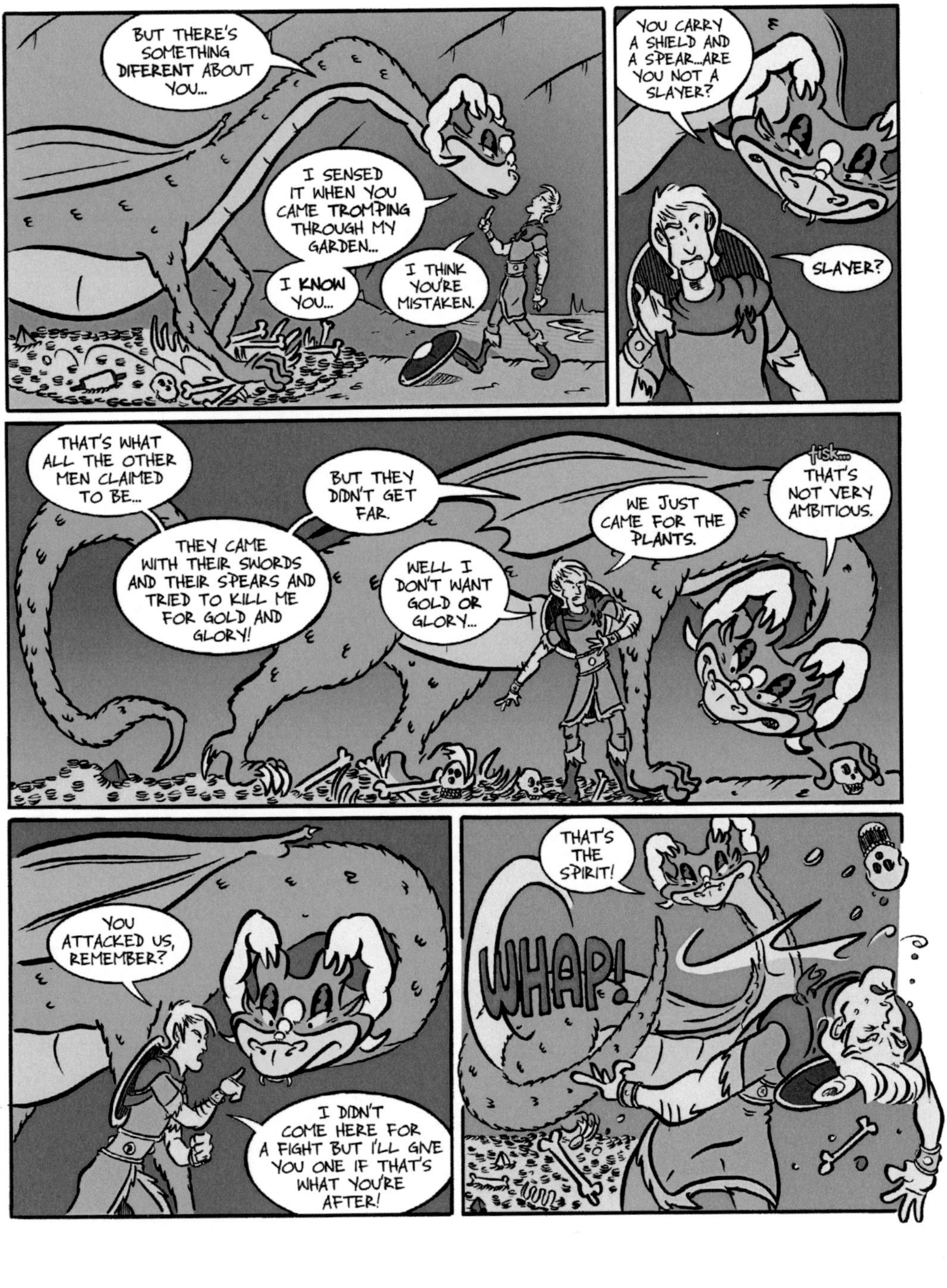
BUT THERE'S SOMETHING DIFERENT ABOUT YOU...
I SENSED IT WHEN YOU CAME TROMPING THROUGH MY GARDEN...
I KNOW YOU...
I THINK YOU'RE MISTAKEN.
YOU CARRY A SHIELD AND A SPEAR...ARE YOU NOT A SLAYER?
SLAYER?
THAT'S WHAT ALL THE OTHER MEN CLAIMED TO BE...
THEY CAME WITH THEIR SWORDS AND THEIR SPEARS AND TRIED TO KILL ME FOR GOLD AND GLORY!
BUT THEY DIDN'T GET FAR.
WELL I DON'T WANT GOLD OR GLORY...
WE JUST CAME FOR THE PLANTS.
fisk...
THAT'S NOT VERY AMBITIOUS.
YOU ATTACKED US, REMEMBER?
I DIDN'T COME HERE FOR A FIGHT BUT I'LL GIVE YOU ONE IF THAT'S WHAT YOU'RE AFTER!
THAT'S THE SPIRIT!
WHAP!

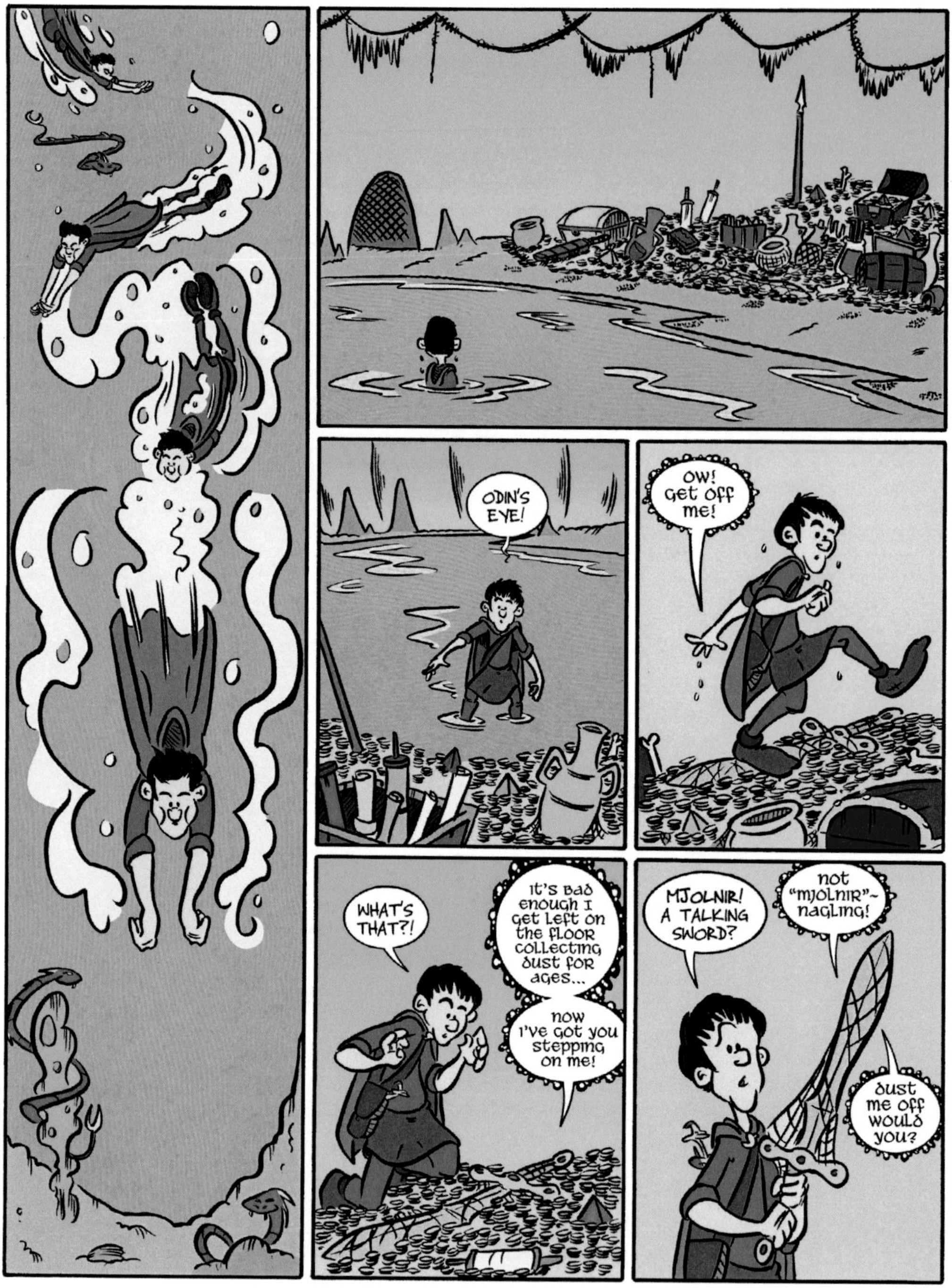
ODIN'S EYE!
OW! Get off me!
WHAT'S THAT?!
It's Bad enough I get Left on the floor collecting dust for ages...
now I've got you stepping on me!
MJOLNIR! A TALKING SWORD?
not "mjolnir"~ nagling!
dust me off would you?

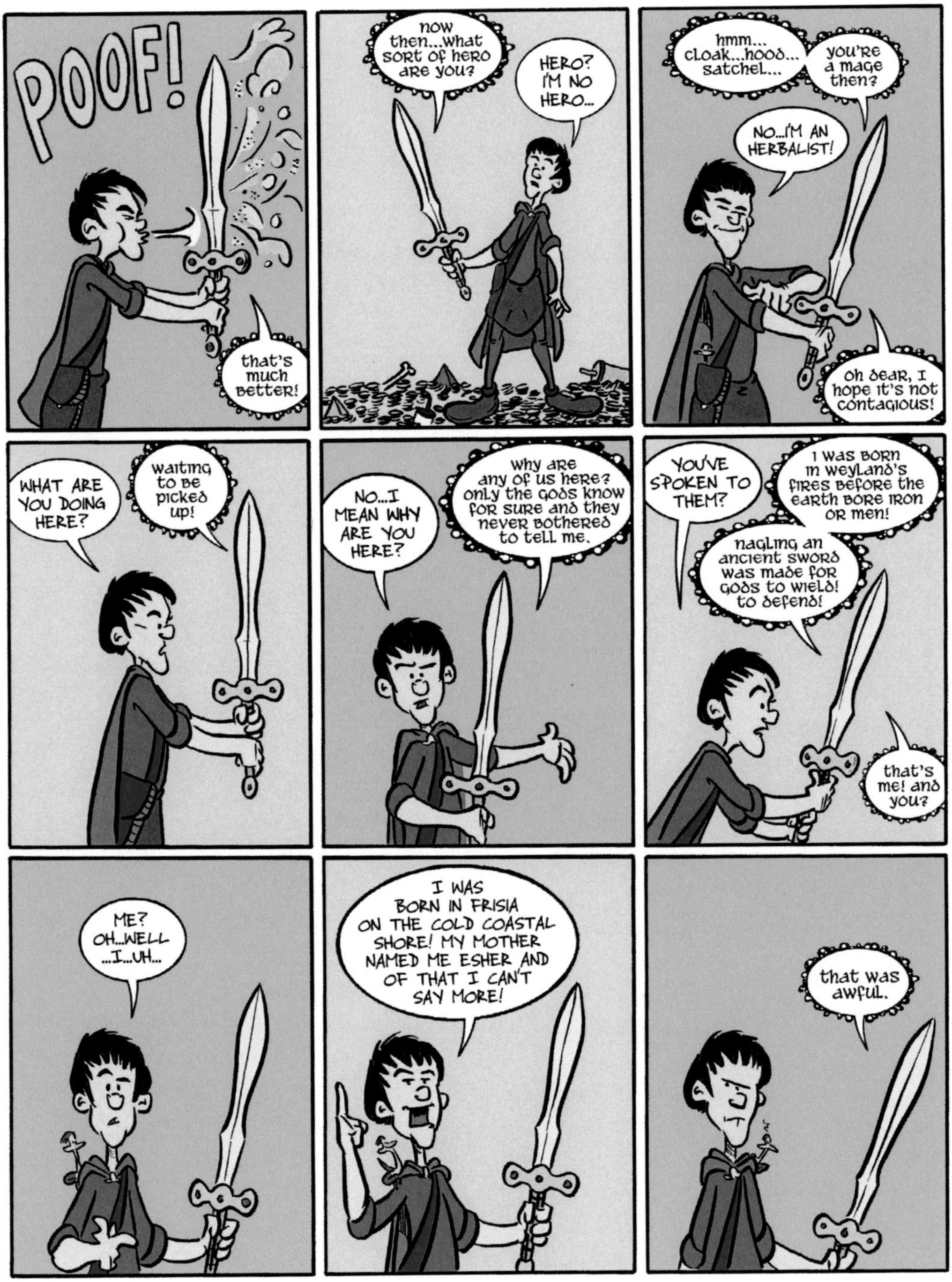
POOF!
that's much better!
now then...what sort of hero are you?
HERO? I'M NO HERO...
hmm... cloak...hood... satchel...
you're a mage then?
NO...I'M AN HERBALIST!
oh dear, I hope it's not contagious!
WHAT ARE YOU DOING HERE?
waiting to be picked up!
NO...I MEAN WHY ARE YOU HERE?
why are any of us here? only the gods know for sure and they never bothered to tell me.
YOU'VE SPOKEN TO THEM?
I was born in weyland's fires before the earth bore iron or men!
nagling an ancient sword was made for gods to wield! to defend!
that's me! and you?
ME? OH...WELL ...I...UH...
I WAS BORN IN FRISIA ON THE COLD COASTAL SHORE! MY MOTHER NAMED ME ESHER AND OF THAT I CAN'T SAY MORE!
that was awful.

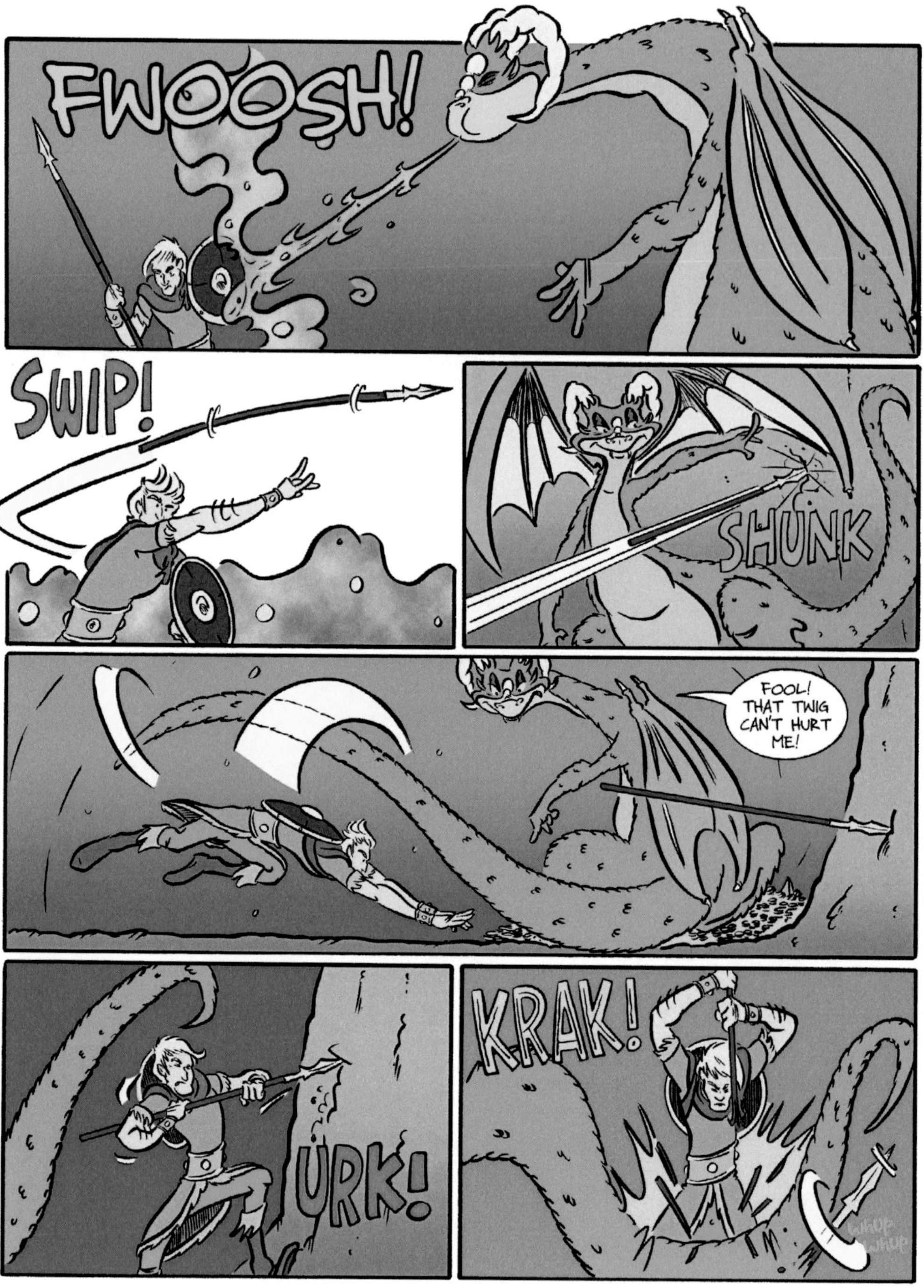
FWOOSH!
SWIP!
SHUNK
FOOL! THAT TWIG CAN'T HURT ME!
URK!
KRAK!
WHUP WHUP

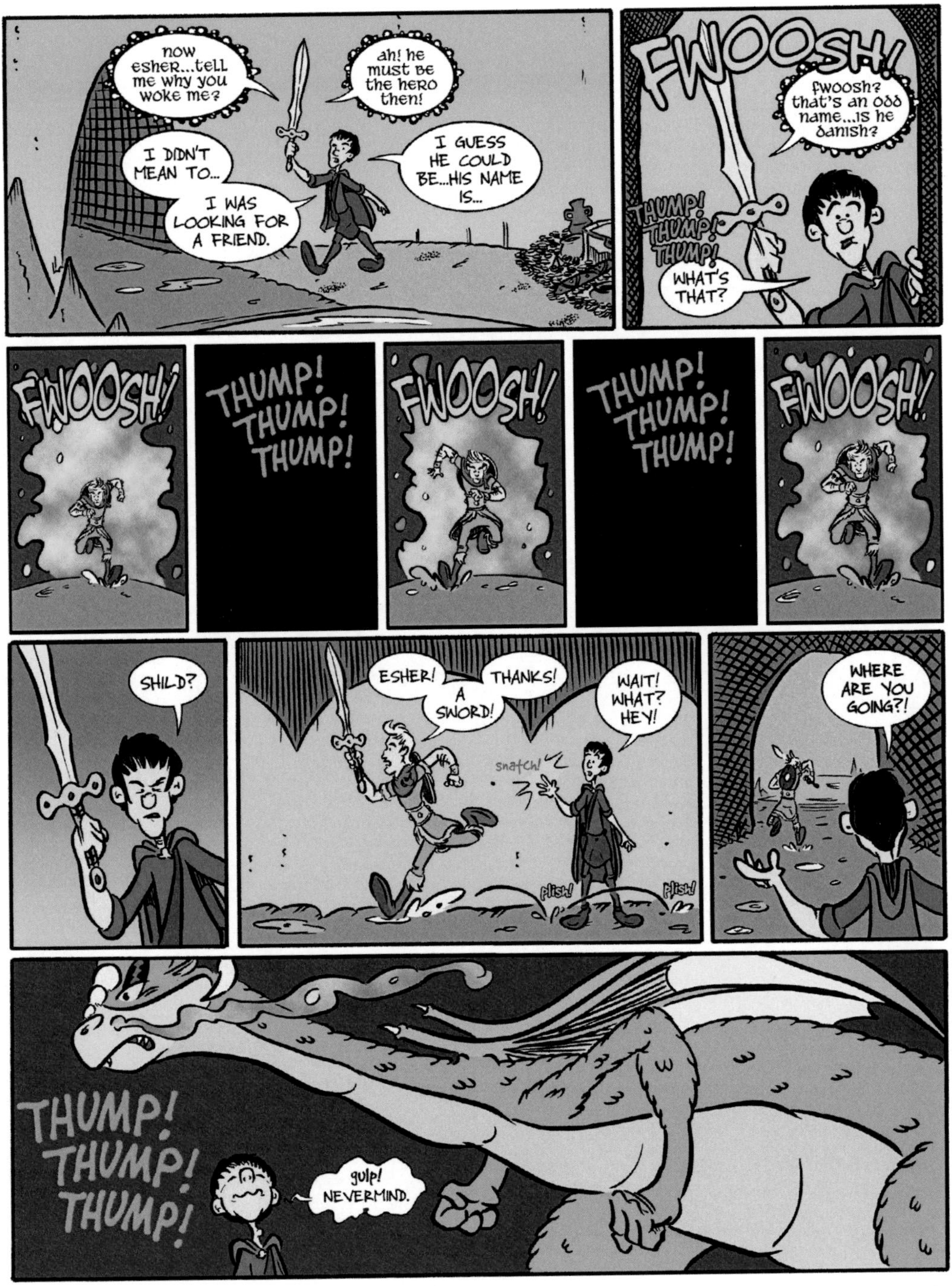
now esher...tell me why you woke me?
ah! he must be the hero then!
I DIDN'T MEAN TO...
I WAS LOOKING FOR A FRIEND.
I GUESS HE COULD BE...HIS NAME IS...
FWOOSH!
fwoosh? that's an odd name...is he danish?
THUMP! THUMP! THUMP!
WHAT'S THAT?
FWOOSH!
THUMP! THUMP! THUMP!
FWOOSH!
THUMP! THUMP! THUMP!
FWOOSH!
SHILD?
ESHER!
A SWORD!
THANKS!
WAIT! WHAT? HEY!
snatch!
plish!
plish!
WHERE ARE YOU GOING?!
THUMP! THUMP! THUMP!
gulp! NEVERMIND.

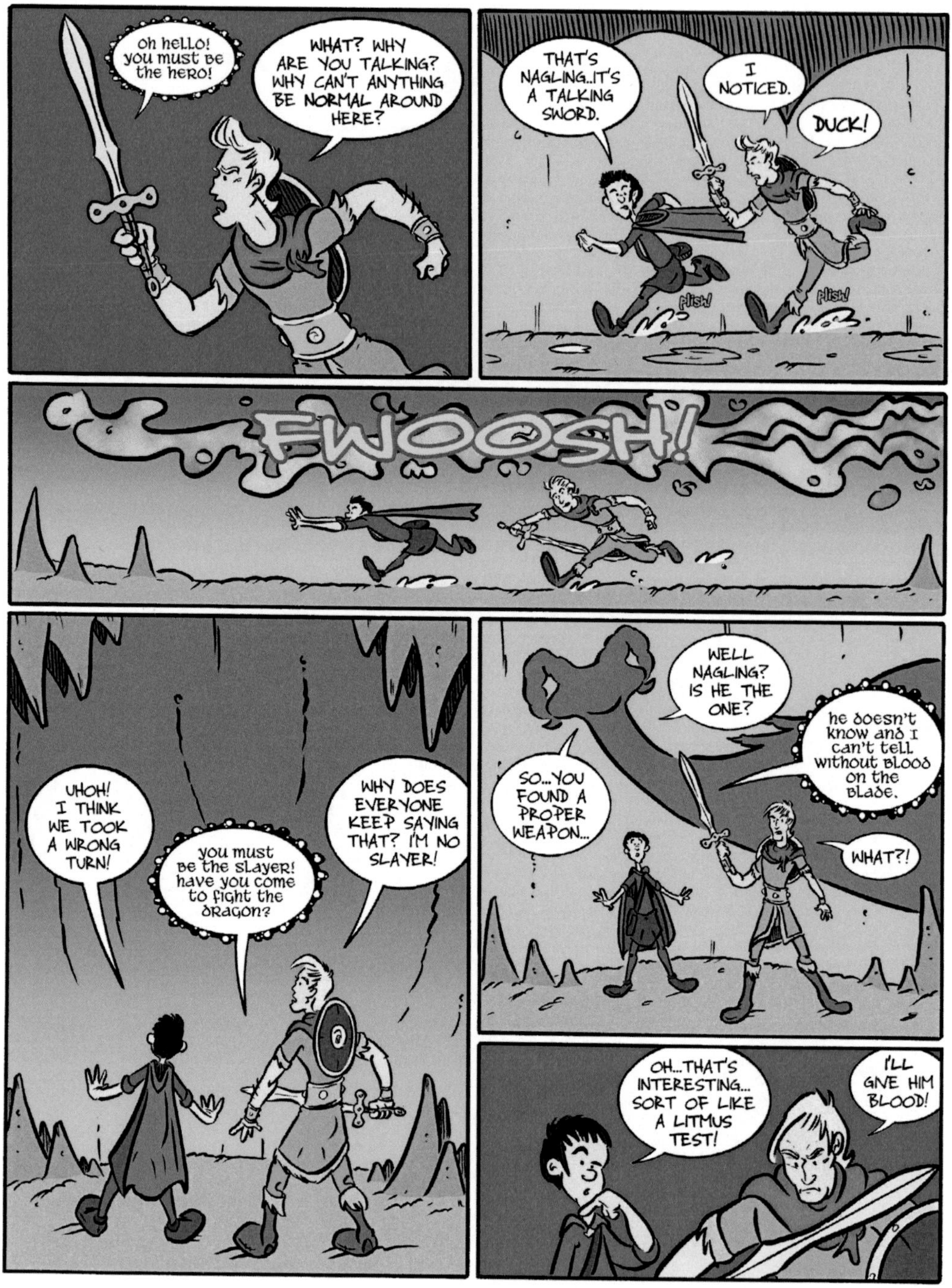
oh hello! you must be the hero!
WHAT? WHY ARE YOU TALKING? WHY CAN'T ANYTHING BE NORMAL AROUND HERE?
THAT'S NAGLING..IT'S A TALKING SWORD.
I NOTICED.
DUCK!
plish!
plish!
FWOOSH!
UHOH! I THINK WE TOOK A WRONG TURN!
you must be the slayer! have you come to fight the dragon?
WHY DOES EVERYONE KEEP SAYING THAT? I'M NO SLAYER!
WELL NAGLING? IS HE THE ONE?
he doesn't know and I can't tell without blood on the blade.
SO...YOU FOUND A PROPER WEAPON...
WHAT?!
OH...THAT'S INTERESTING... SORT OF LIKE A LITMUS TEST!
I'LL GIVE HIM BLOOD!

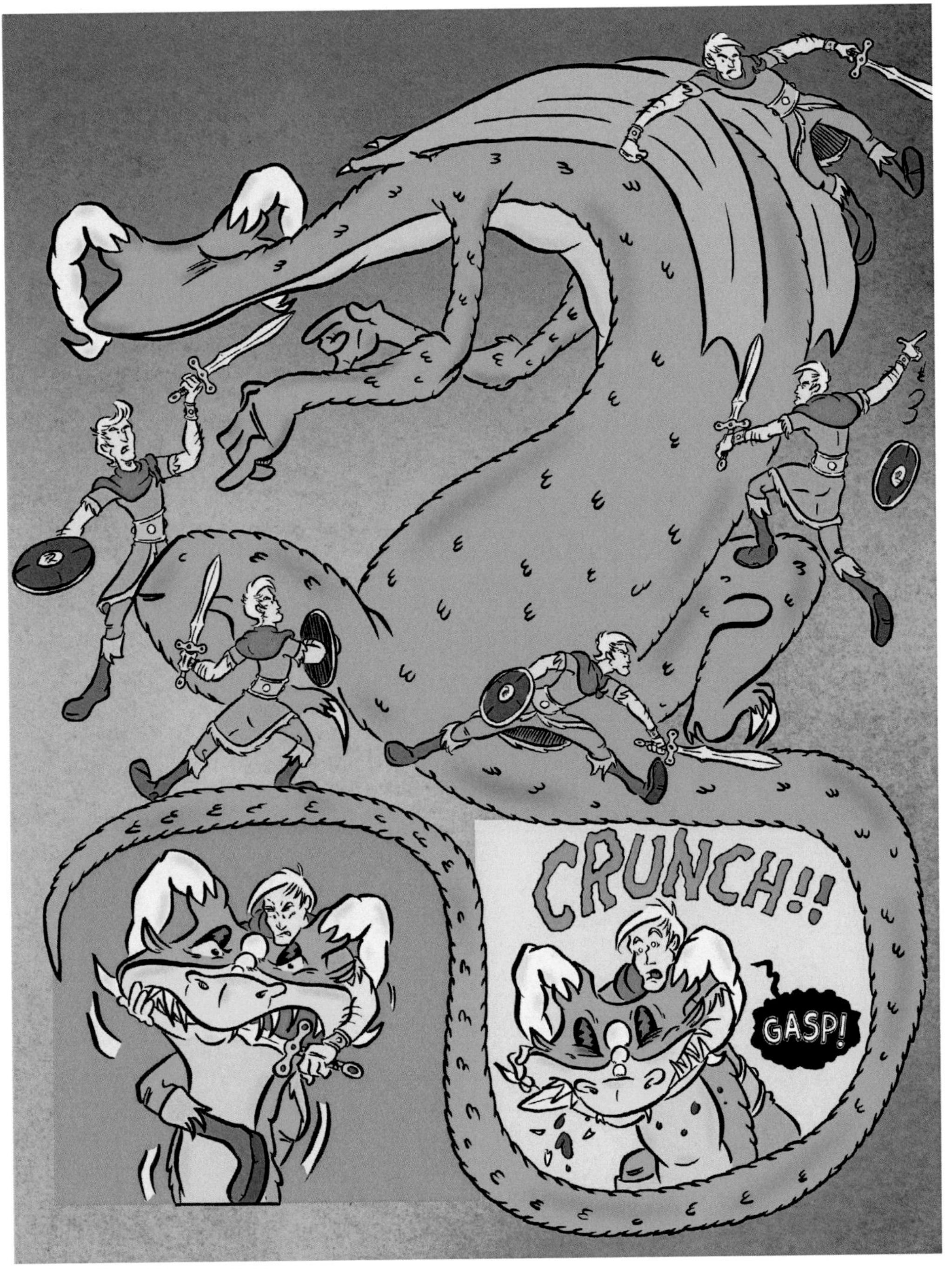
CRUNCH!!
GASP!

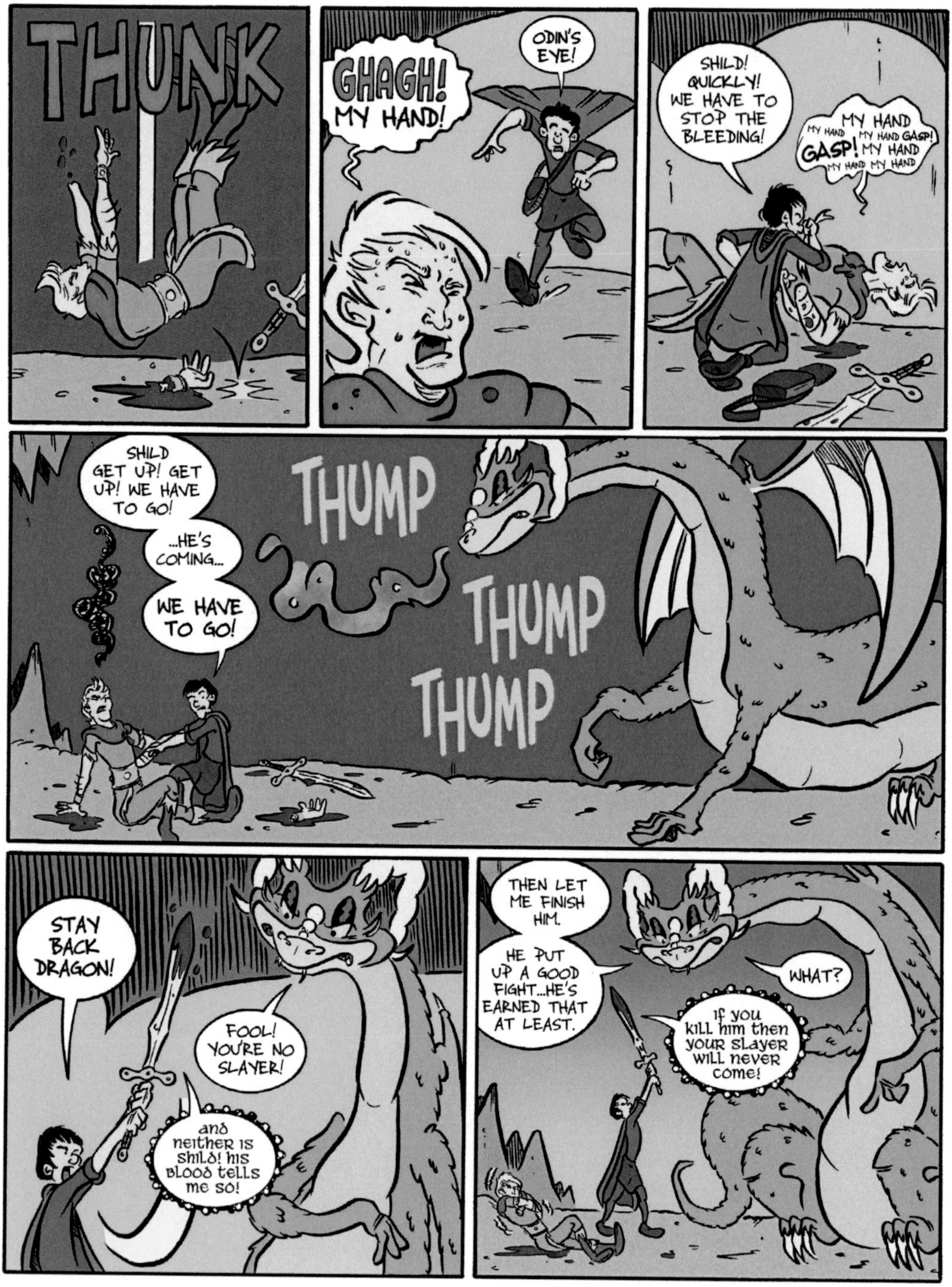
THUNK
GHAGH! MY HAND!
ODIN'S EYE!
SHILD! QUICKLY! WE HAVE TO STOP THE BLEEDING!
MY HAND MY HAND MY HAND GASP! GASP! MY HAND MY HAND MY HAND
SHILD GET UP! GET UP! WE HAVE TO GO!
...HE'S COMING...
WE HAVE TO GO!
THUMP
THUMP
THUMP
STAY BACK DRAGON!
FOOL! YOU'RE NO SLAYER!
and neither is shild! his blood tells me so!
THEN LET ME FINISH HIM.
HE PUT UP A GOOD FIGHT...HE'S EARNED THAT AT LEAST.
WHAT?
if you kill him then your slayer will never come!

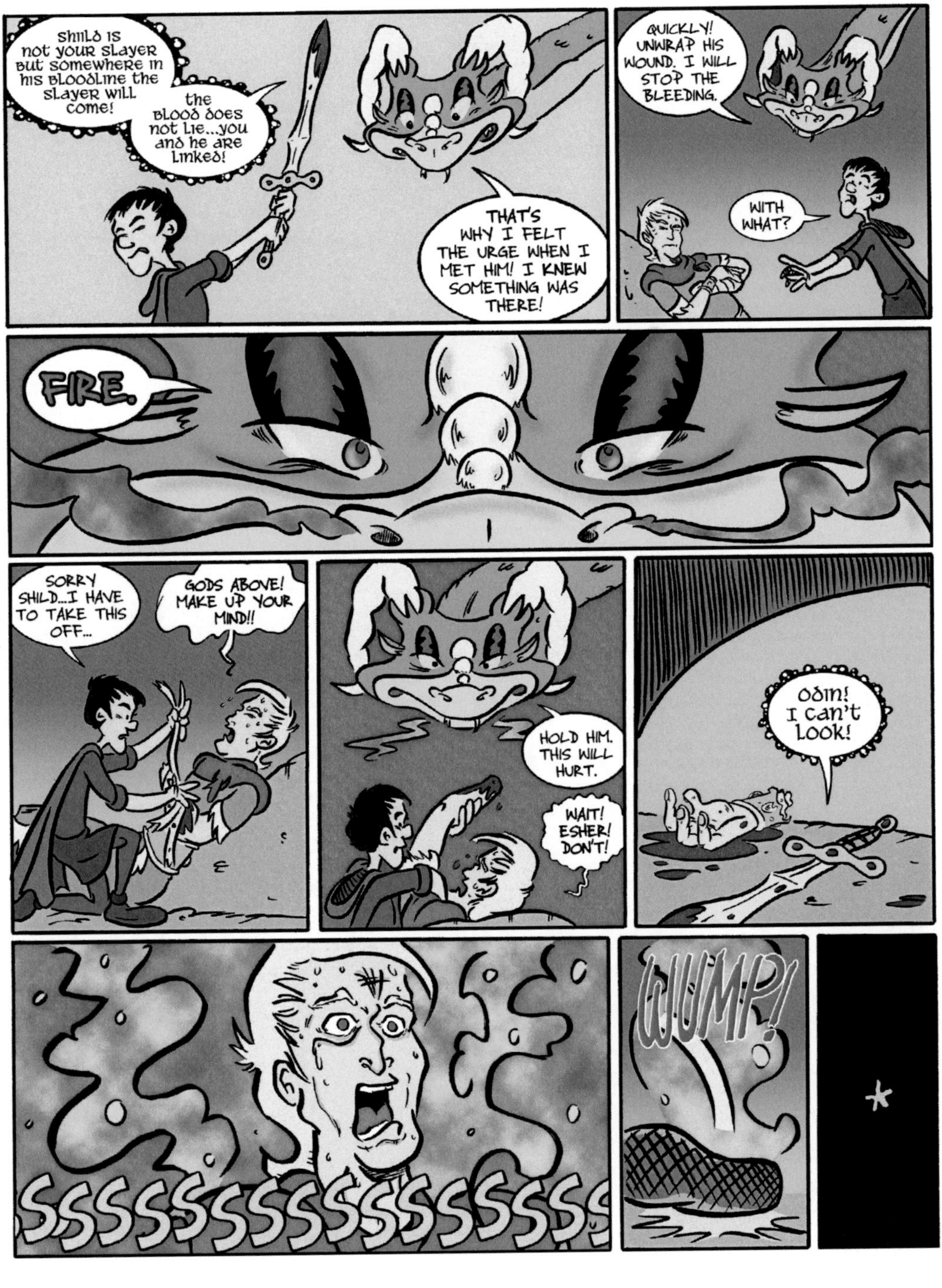
shild is not your slayer but somewhere in his bloodline the slayer will come!
the blood does not lie...you and he are linked!
THAT'S WHY I FELT THE URGE WHEN I MET HIM! I KNEW SOMETHING WAS THERE!
QUICKLY! UNWRAP HIS WOUND. I WILL STOP THE BLEEDING.
WITH WHAT?
FIRE.
SORRY SHILD...I HAVE TO TAKE THIS OFF...
GODS ABOVE! MAKE UP YOUR MIND!!
HOLD HIM. THIS WILL HURT.
WAIT! ESHER! DON'T!
odin! I can't look!
SSSSSSSSSSSSSSSSSS
WUMP!
*

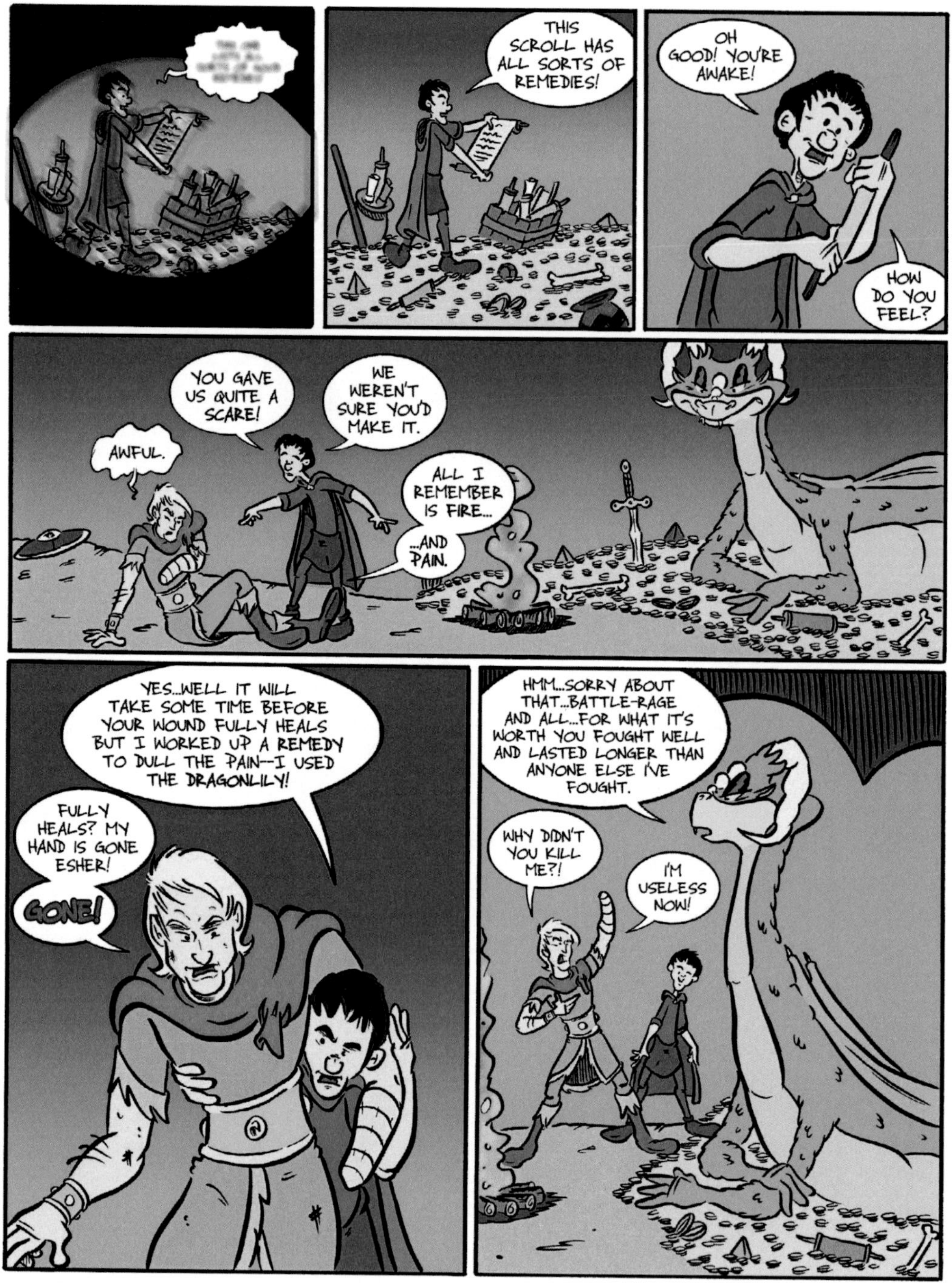
THIS SCROLL HAS ALL SORTS OF REMEDIES!
OH GOOD! YOU'RE AWAKE!
HOW DO YOU FEEL?
AWFUL.
YOU GAVE US QUITE A SCARE!
WE WEREN'T SURE YOU'D MAKE IT.
ALL I REMEMBER IS FIRE...
...AND PAIN.
YES...WELL IT WILL TAKE SOME TIME BEFORE YOUR WOUND FULLY HEALS BUT I WORKED UP A REMEDY TO DULL THE PAIN--I USED THE DRAGONLILY!
FULLY HEALS? MY HAND IS GONE ESHER!
GONE!
HMM...SORRY ABOUT THAT...BATTLE-RAGE AND ALL...FOR WHAT IT'S WORTH YOU FOUGHT WELL AND LASTED LONGER THAN ANYONE ELSE I'VE FOUGHT.
WHY DIDN'T YOU KILL ME?!
I'M USELESS NOW!

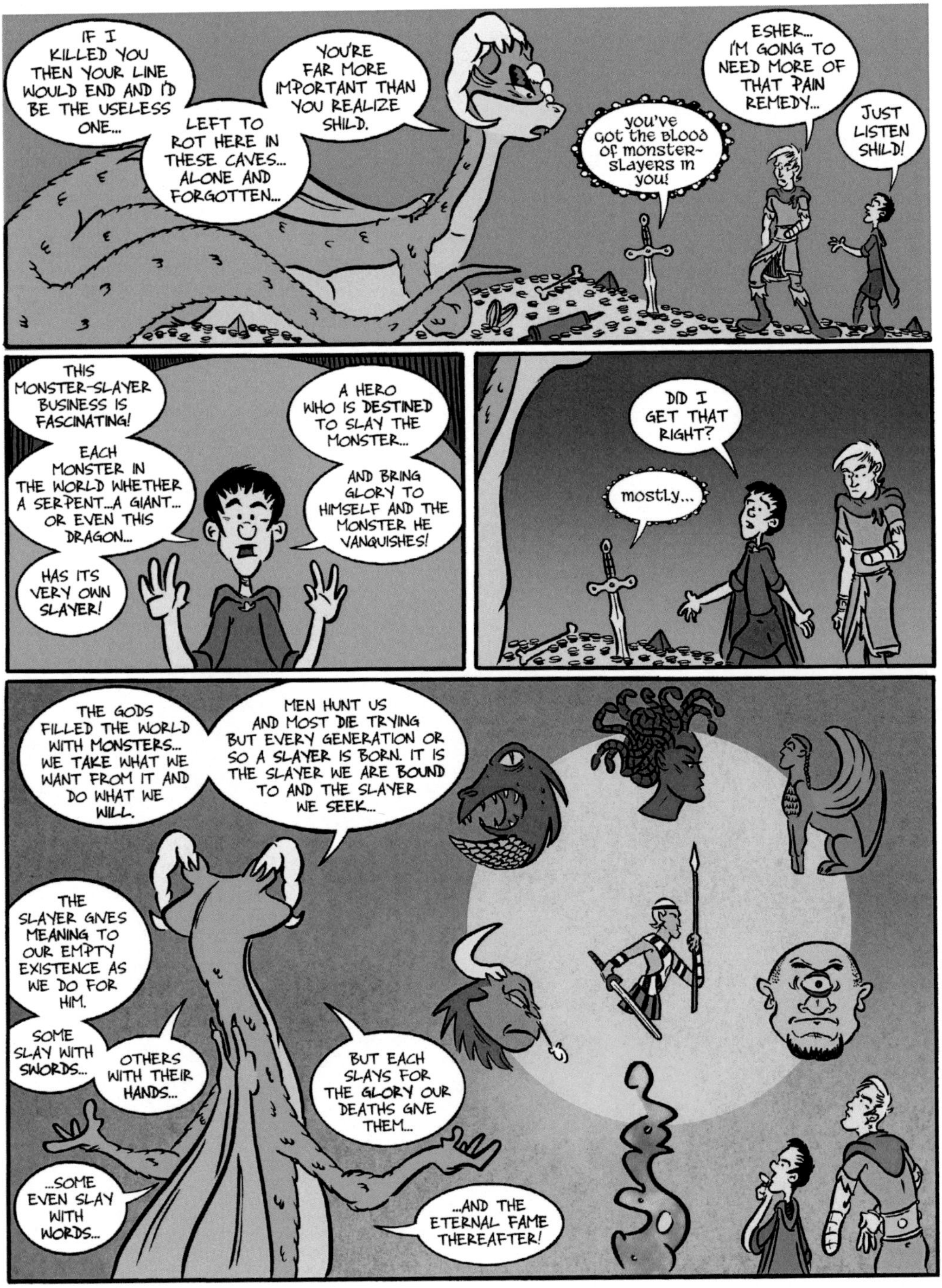
IF I KILLED YOU THEN YOUR LINE WOULD END AND I'D BE THE USELESS ONE...
LEFT TO ROT HERE IN THESE CAVES... ALONE AND FORGOTTEN...
YOU'RE FAR MORE IMPORTANT THAN YOU REALIZE SHILD.
you've got the blood of monster-slayers in you!
ESHER... I'M GOING TO NEED MORE OF THAT PAIN REMEDY...
JUST LISTEN SHILD!
THIS MONSTER-SLAYER BUSINESS IS FASCINATING!
EACH MONSTER IN THE WORLD WHETHER A SERPENT...A GIANT... OR EVEN THIS DRAGON...
HAS ITS VERY OWN SLAYER!
A HERO WHO IS DESTINED TO SLAY THE MONSTER...
AND BRING GLORY TO HIMSELF AND THE MONSTER HE VANQUISHES!
DID I GET THAT RIGHT?
mostly...
THE GODS FILLED THE WORLD WITH MONSTERS... WE TAKE WHAT WE WANT FROM IT AND DO WHAT WE WILL.
MEN HUNT US AND MOST DIE TRYING BUT EVERY GENERATION OR SO A SLAYER IS BORN. IT IS THE SLAYER WE ARE BOUND TO AND THE SLAYER WE SEEK...
THE SLAYER GIVES MEANING TO OUR EMPTY EXISTENCE AS WE DO FOR HIM.
SOME SLAY WITH SWORDS...
OTHERS WITH THEIR HANDS...
BUT EACH SLAYS FOR THE GLORY OUR DEATHS GIVE THEM...
...SOME EVEN SLAY WITH WORDS...
...AND THE ETERNAL FAME THEREAFTER!

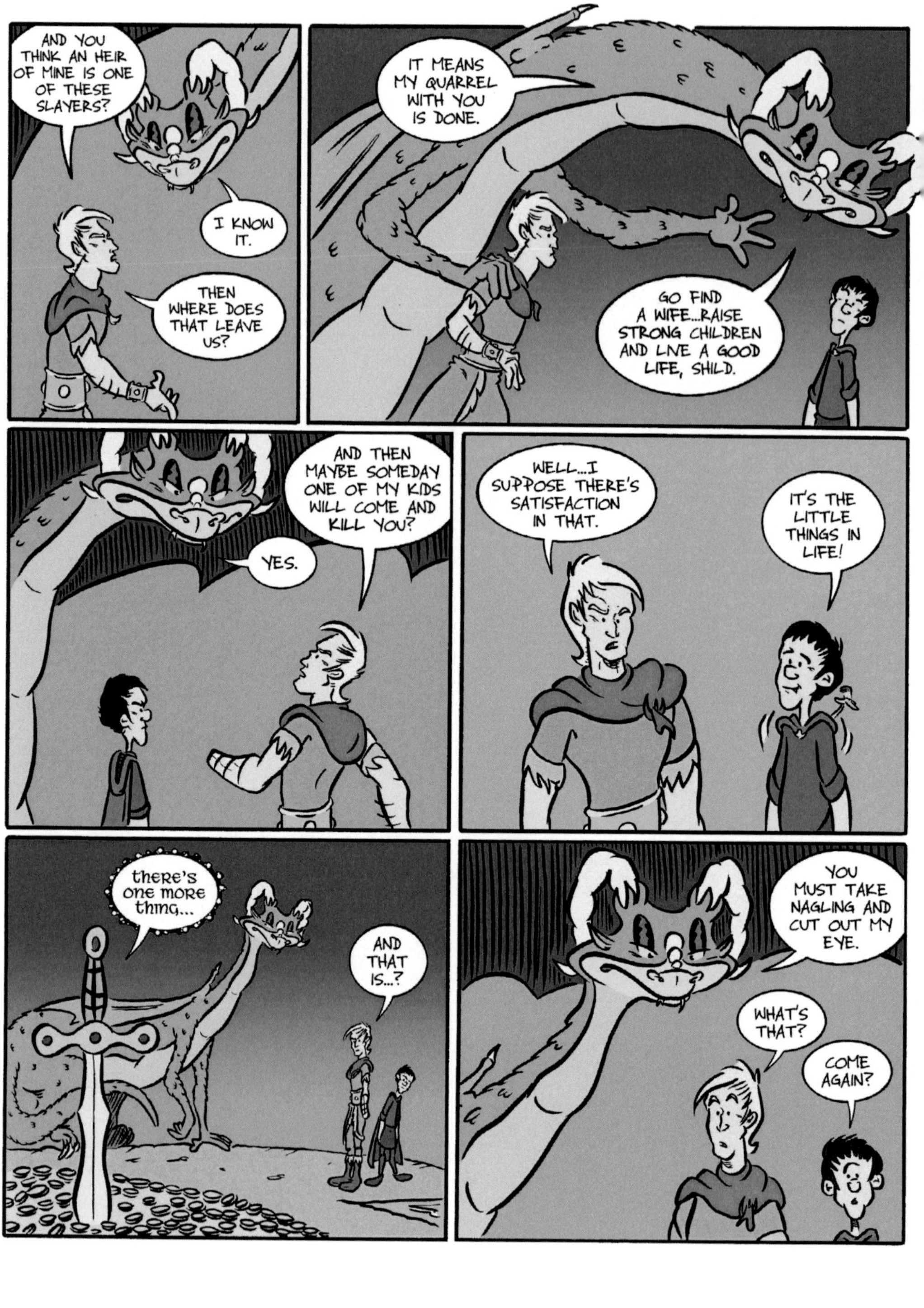
AND YOU THINK AN HEIR OF MINE IS ONE OF THESE SLAYERS?
I KNOW IT.
THEN WHERE DOES THAT LEAVE US?
IT MEANS MY QUARREL WITH YOU IS DONE.
GO FIND A WIFE...RAISE STRONG CHILDREN AND LIVE A GOOD LIFE, SHILD.
AND THEN MAYBE SOMEDAY ONE OF MY KIDS WILL COME AND KILL YOU?
YES.
WELL...I SUPPOSE THERE'S SATISFACTION IN THAT.
IT'S THE LITTLE THINGS IN LIFE!
there's one more thing...
AND THAT IS...?
YOU MUST TAKE NAGLING AND CUT OUT MY EYE.
WHAT'S THAT?
COME AGAIN?

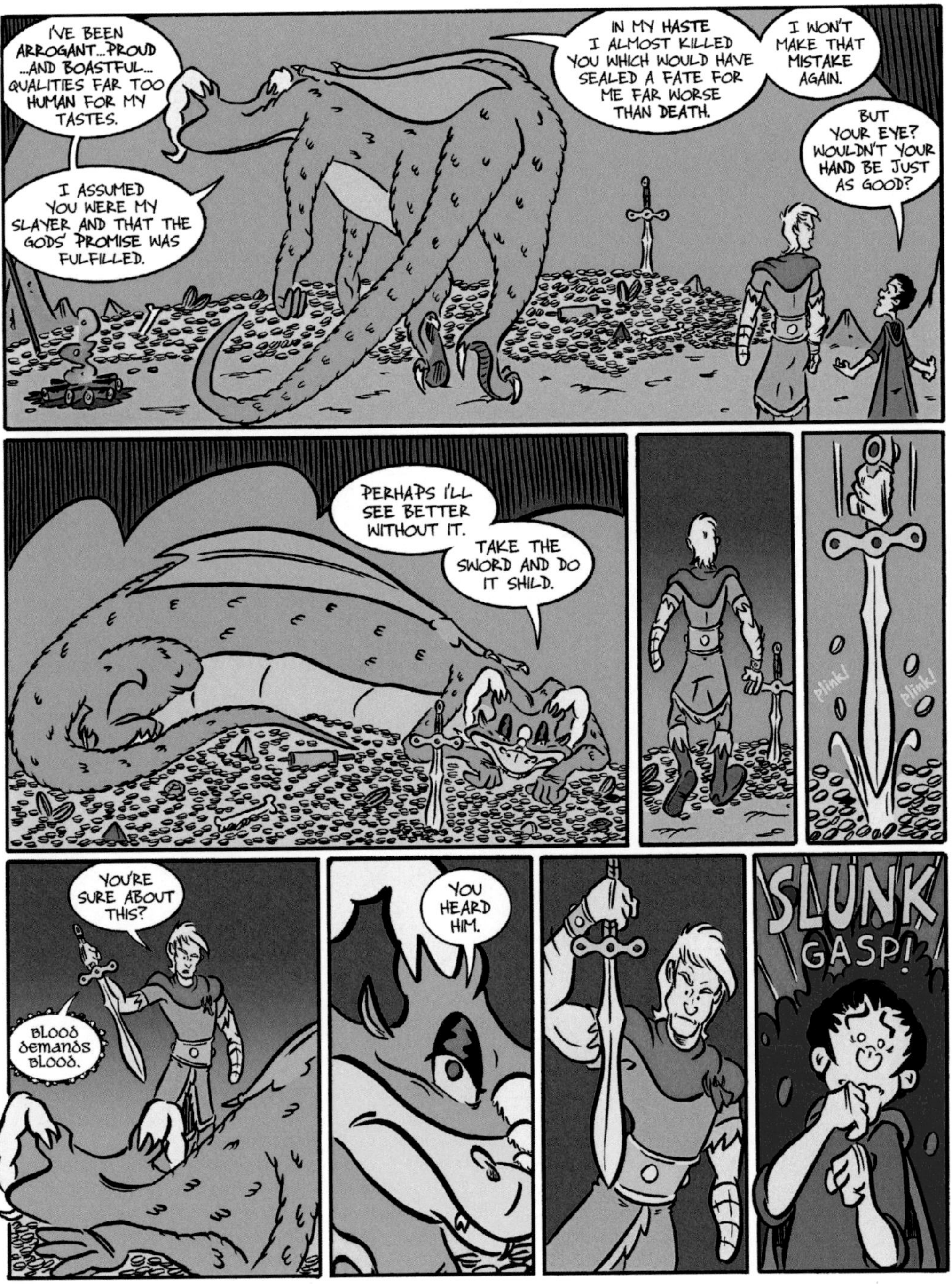
I'VE BEEN ARROGANT...PROUD ...AND BOASTFUL... QUALITIES FAR TOO HUMAN FOR MY TASTES.
I ASSUMED YOU WERE MY SLAYER AND THAT THE GODS' PROMISE WAS FULFILLED.
IN MY HASTE I ALMOST KILLED YOU WHICH WOULD HAVE SEALED A FATE FOR ME FAR WORSE THAN DEATH.
I WON'T MAKE THAT MISTAKE AGAIN.
BUT YOUR EYE? WOULDN'T YOUR HAND BE JUST AS GOOD?
PERHAPS I'LL SEE BETTER WITHOUT IT.
TAKE THE SWORD AND DO IT SHILD.
plink!
plink!
YOU'RE SURE ABOUT THIS?
BLOOD DEMANDS BLOOD.
YOU HEARD HIM.
SLUNK
GASP!

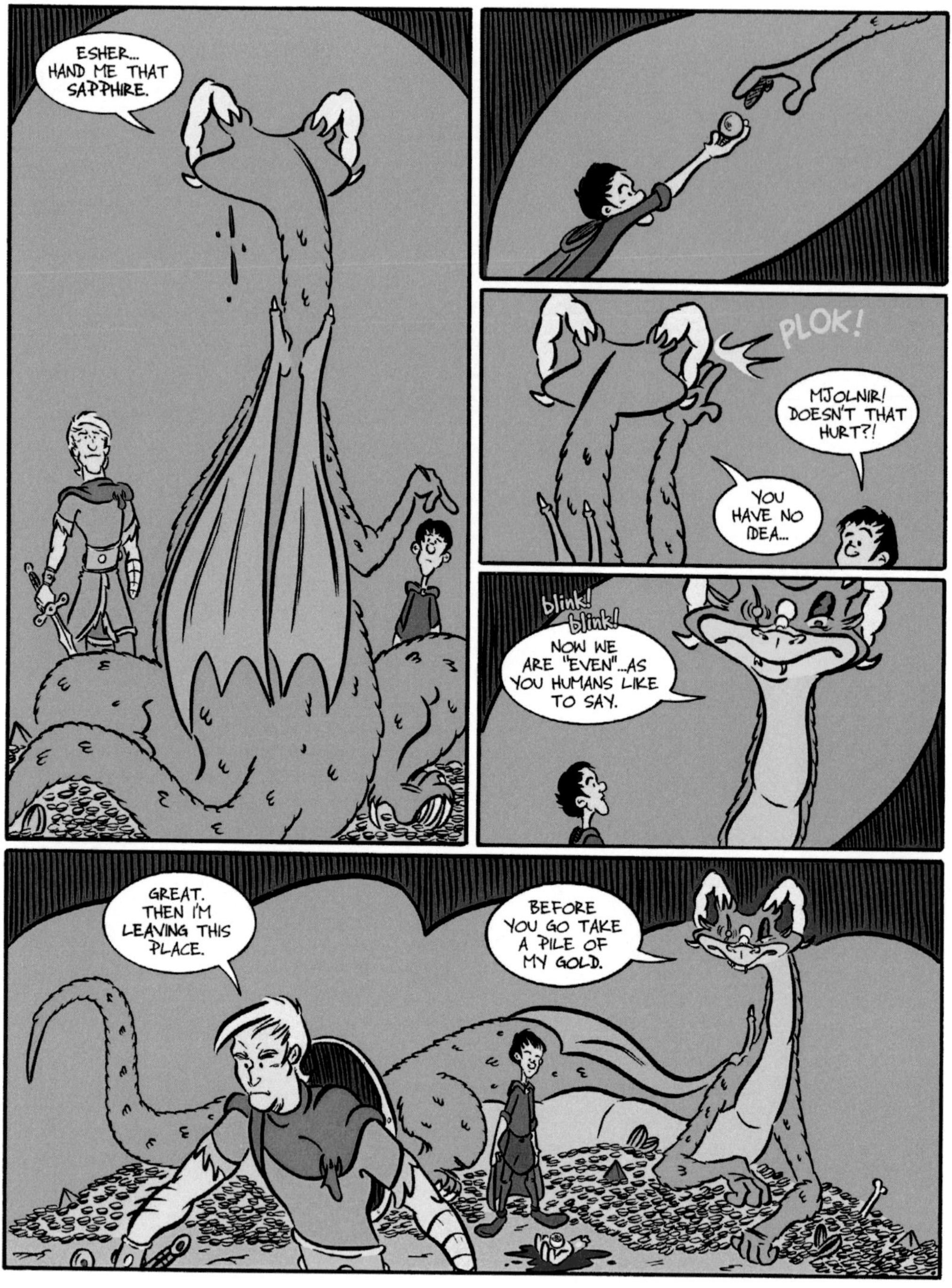
ESHER... HAND ME THAT SAPPHIRE.
PLOK!
MJOLNIR! DOESN'T THAT HURT?!
YOU HAVE NO IDEA...
blink! blink!
NOW WE ARE "EVEN"...AS YOU HUMANS LIKE TO SAY.
GREAT. THEN I'M LEAVING THIS PLACE.
BEFORE YOU GO TAKE A PILE OF MY GOLD.

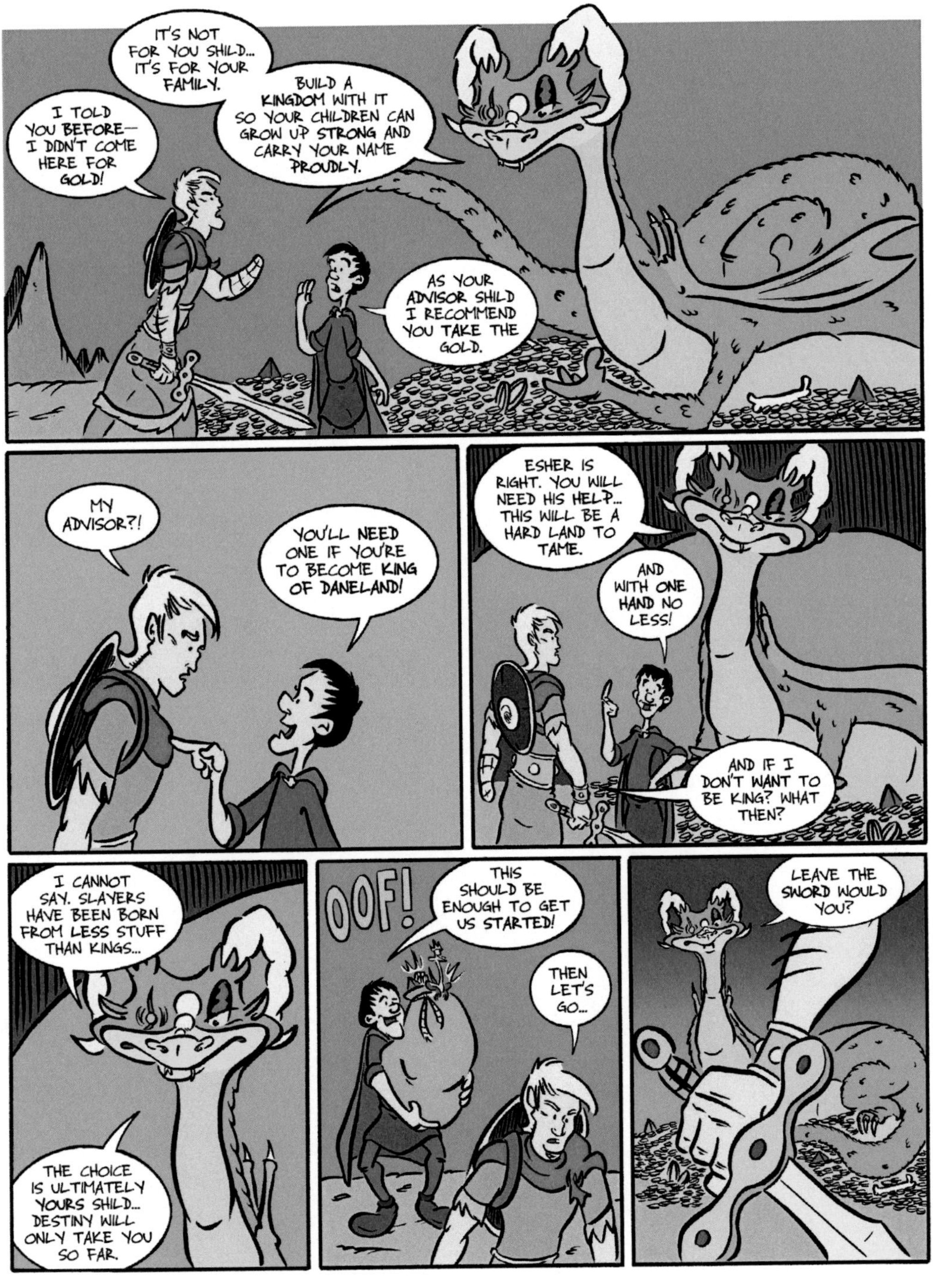
I TOLD YOU BEFORE— I DIDN'T COME HERE FOR GOLD!
IT'S NOT FOR YOU SHILD... IT'S FOR YOUR FAMILY.
BUILD A KINGDOM WITH IT SO YOUR CHILDREN CAN GROW UP STRONG AND CARRY YOUR NAME PROUDLY.
AS YOUR ADVISOR SHILD I RECOMMEND YOU TAKE THE GOLD.
MY ADVISOR?!
YOU'LL NEED ONE IF YOU'RE TO BECOME KING OF DANELAND!
ESHER IS RIGHT. YOU WILL NEED HIS HELP... THIS WILL BE A HARD LAND TO TAME.
AND WITH ONE HAND NO LESS!
AND IF I DON'T WANT TO BE KING? WHAT THEN?
I CANNOT SAY. SLAYERS HAVE BEEN BORN FROM LESS STUFF THAN KINGS...
THE CHOICE IS ULTIMATELY YOURS SHILD... DESTINY WILL ONLY TAKE YOU SO FAR.
OOF!
THIS SHOULD BE ENOUGH TO GET US STARTED!
THEN LET'S GO...
LEAVE THE SWORD WOULD YOU?

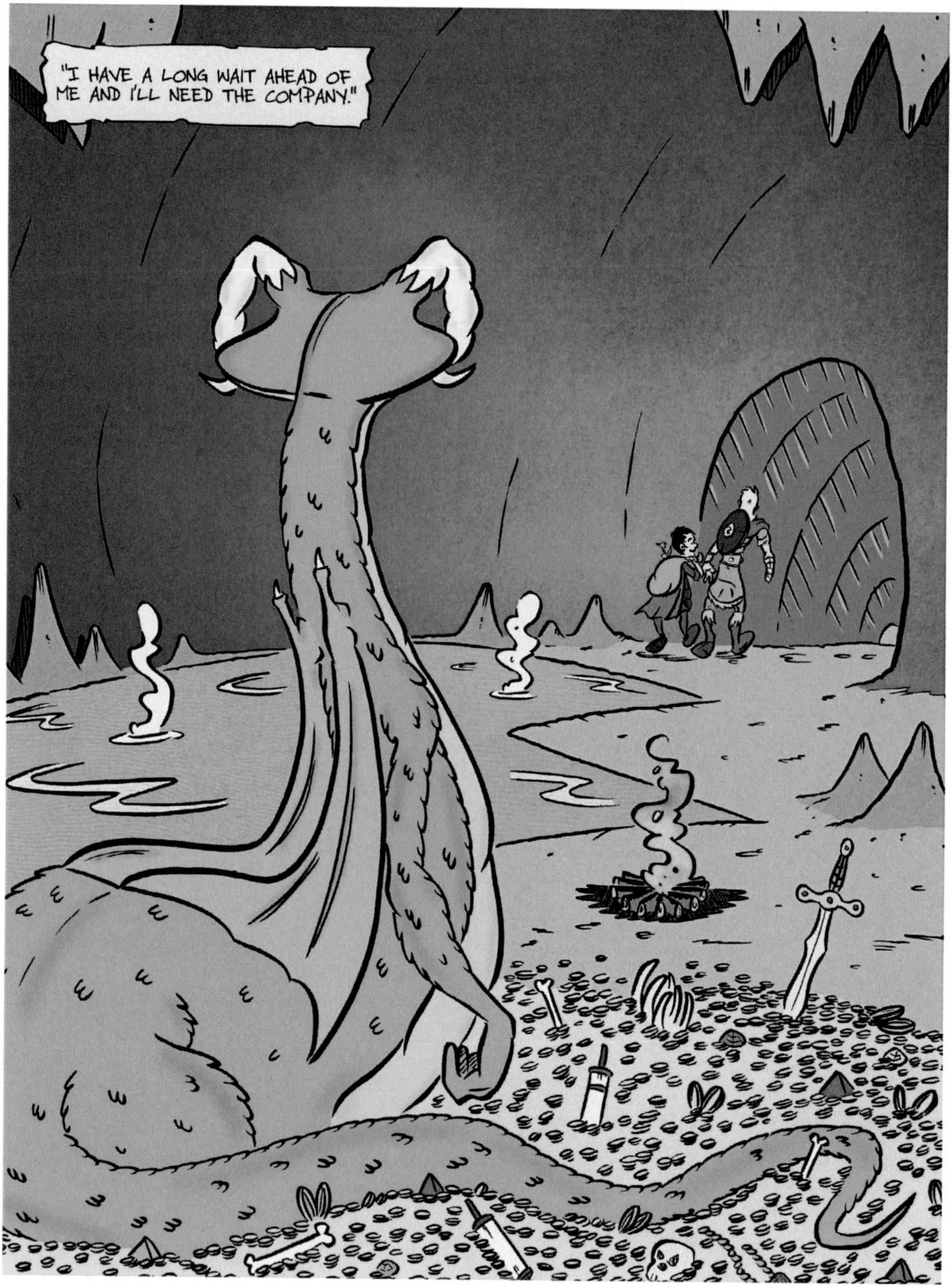
"I HAVE A LONG WAIT AHEAD OF ME AND I'LL NEED THE COMPANY."

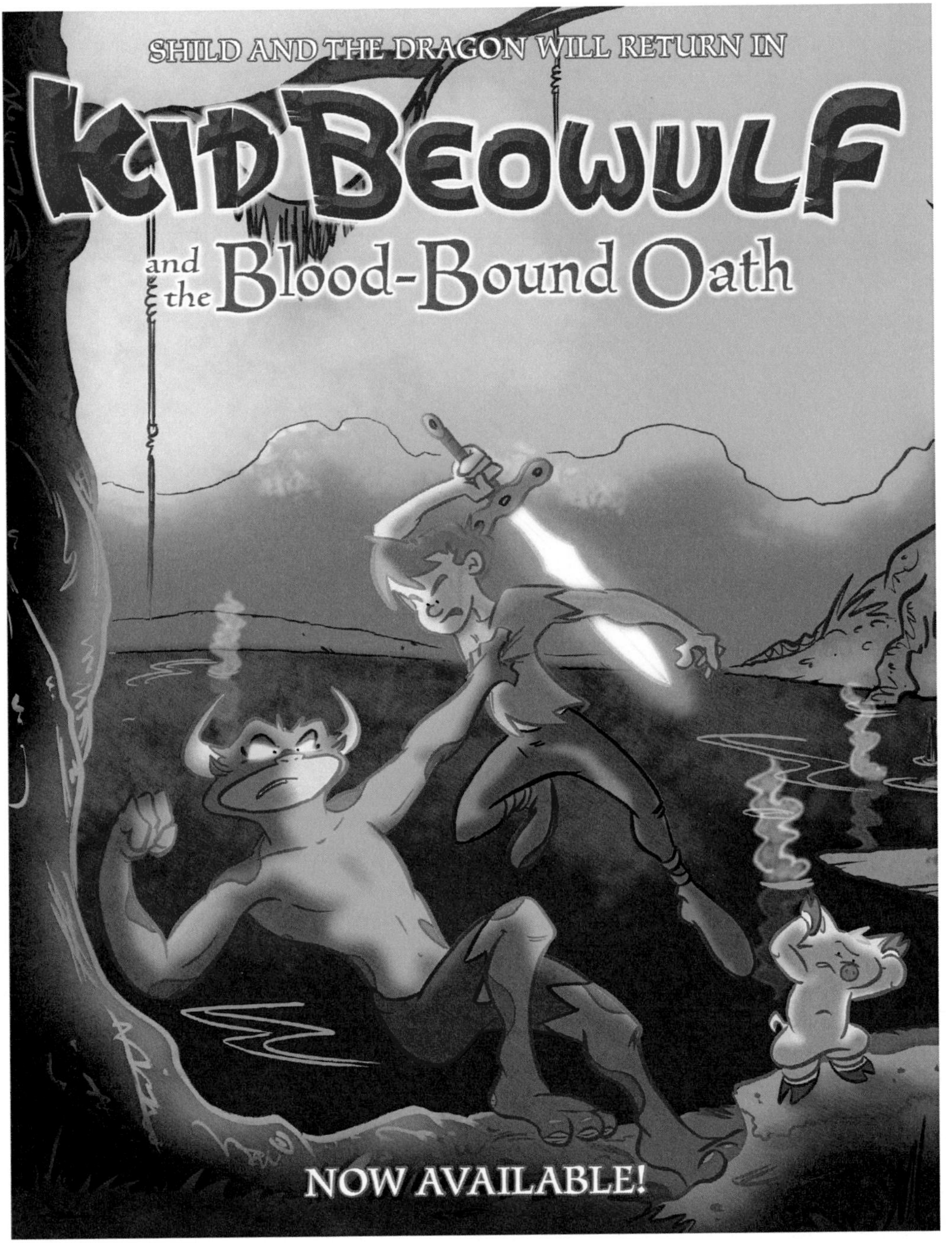
SHILD AND THE DRAGON WILL RETURN IN
KID BEOWULF
and the Blood-Bound Oath
NOW AVAILABLE!

KID BEOWULF CATALOGUE

KID BEOWULF
and the Blood-Bound Oath
Alexis E. Fajardo

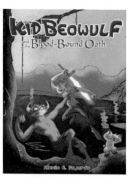

Book 1: *Kid Beowulf and the Blood-Bound Oath*

The heroes' destiny is tied to the past when a prince begins a quest for power that leads him to a fiery dragon, an enchanted sword, and an oath sworn in blood. Discover the extraordinary origin of twin brothers Beowulf and Grendel!
$15.95 – Grades 6 & up – B&W, 7 x 9 – 208 pgs
ISBN 978-0-9801419-1-7

KID BEOWULF
And The SONG of ROLAND
Alexis E. Fajardo

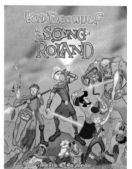

Book 2: *Kid Beowulf and the Song of Roland*

Beowulf and Grendel trek to France and discover a country in peril: King Charlemagne is ailing, his knights are exiled and the hero Roland needs a kick in the pants! Can Beowulf and Grendel unite France before it is taken over by an invading Saracen horde?
$17.95 – Grades 6 & up – B&W, 7 x 9 – 272 pgs
ISBN 978-0-9801419-2-4

KID BEOWULF
and the Rise of
EL CID
Alexis E. Fajardo

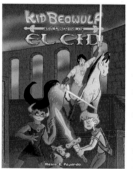

Book 3: *Kid Beowulf and the Rise of El Cid*

Beowulf and Grendel are in war torn Spain, where honor is hard fought, allegiances are dubious, and the bulls run wild! Amidst it all comes a young knight named Rodrigo, who fights for the name he has lost, the land he loves, and the virtue they have both forgotten.

$14.95 – Grades 6 & up – B&W, 7 x 9 – 250 pgs
ISBN 978-0-9746000-6-2

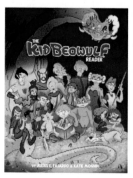

THE
KID BEOWULF
READER
BY ALEXIS E. FAJARDO & KATIE MONNIN

The Kid Beowulf Reader

Part classroom guide and part historiography, this book is full of fun and insight on the creation of the first trilogy. The reader also features lesson plans and discussion questions for the teachers using Kid Beowulf in class.

$12.00 – Grades 6 & up – BW, 7x9 –240pgs
ISBN 978-09746000-4-8

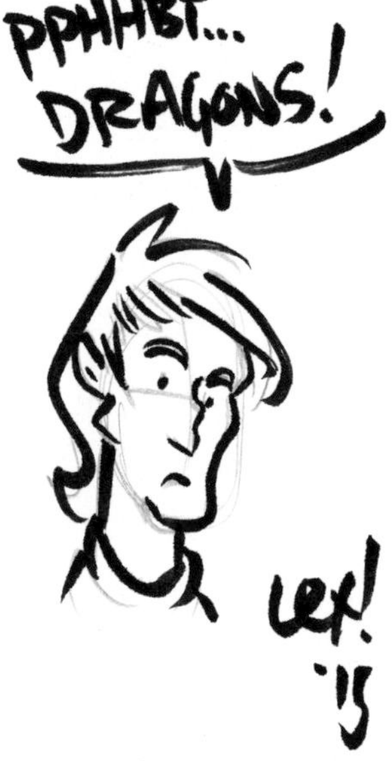
PPHHBT...
DRAGONS!
LEX!
'15

18300018R00024

Made in the USA
San Bernardino, CA
09 January 2015